Hey, Wait a minute!
The critics LOVE

Hey, Wait a Minute
(I wrote a book!)

"The ex-coach comes across as the lovable leader of a merry band of Hell's Angels in shoulder pads, once known as the Oakland Raiders."

Los Angeles Times

"Good news for John Madden fans: The old coach-turned-broadcaster has written a book. Better news for John Madden fans: He writes the way he talks when he's doing Sunday NFL games for CBS. Boom! Boom! Boom!... Madden reveals a great deal about himself. ... Hey, this is a great little book! Boom! Boom! Boom!"

San Diego Tribune

"In these days of sports books that have nothing nice to say about owners, players, the sporting media or game officials, it's refreshing to read the tales of John Madden.... an entertaining, quick read."

The Pittsburgh Press

(more)

"Like Madden, the book is simple, rambunctious, funny and charming. It is no philosophic treatise but contains many insights, most of them humorous, about the men-children of professional athletics....When the reader finishes it, he finds himself wishing there were more."

Phoenix Republic

"Nobody loves a ghostwriter, but in John Madden's breezy, impudent autobiography, *Hey, Wait a Minute*, everybody should. Dave Anderson is the unsung hero here. He succeeds admirably because he puts no words into the choleric coach's mouth.... Anderson has caught the sound of Madden perfectly—there is no sentence in *Hey, Wait a Minute* that doesn't ring precisely true. Anderson—doubtless sifting through hours of tapes—has shown admirable editing sense in preserving the essence of the man, without allowing the reminiscences to become repetitive."

Cincinnati Enquirer

"In the world of television, with its plastic 'personalities' and 'memorable moments,' its skin-deep character and manufactured emotion, John Madden is something rare and distinctive: The genuine article....Madden is, as this enjoyable little book makes clear, one of those rare people who have been blessed with an absolutely clear view of themselves; he likes being popular and admired, but he doesn't need any of that to tell him who he is."

Jonathan Yardley
The Washington Post

"Madden tells all—from locker room anecdotes to behind-the-scenes stories from the broadcast booth. Madden talks about his most memorable practical jokes, most disastrous calls as Raiders coach and his unconventional disciplinary techniques."

USA Today

"John Madden...has done a lot of things well, but probably what he does best is talk. And now many of the words he spoke into a tape recorder have been set down in print....Like Madden, the book is not pretentious. It does not try to masquerade as scandalous revelation nor banquet-cliché inspiration. It is simply conversationally casual, as informal as Madden holding court in the club car....The stories come fast and ramble through such diverse subjects as Super Bowls, fear of flying, filming Miller Lite commercials, and coaching an outlaw team....Not especially deep. But then Madden himself might suggest, hey, wait a minute, this isn't brain surgery; it's only football."

Philadelphia Inquirer

"Madden talks to you—just as he talks to you on television or in banquet speeches; just, presumably, as he would talk to you over a Miller Lite. Sometimes funny. Sometimes insightful. And consistently captivating...Page after page, Madden shares an array of harmless, behind-the-scenes anecdotes from the locker rooms, sidelines, broadcast booths, Miller Lite taping sessions and other vantage points of his life."

Atlanta Journal Constitution

Hey, Wait a Minute
(I wrote a book!)

John Madden
with Dave Anderson

BALLANTINE BOOKS • NEW YORK

Library of Congress Catalog Card Number: 84-40175

ISBN 0-345-32507-9

This edition published by arrangement with Villard Books

Manufactured in the United States of America

First Ballantine Books Edition: September 1985

To Virginia, Mike and Joe

Contents

1

It's Not a Show

I WAS WILD. MY TEAM, THE OAKLAND RAIDERS, had just lost our 1974 season opener to the Bills, 21–20, in Buffalo on a Monday night. More had happened in the last two minutes than happens to some teams in two games. We had been ahead, 13–7, until the Bills' quarterback, Joe Ferguson, hit Ahmad Rashad with an 8-yard touchdown pass with 1 minute, 59 seconds left. After the kick-off, Jim Braxton of the Bills fumbled, Art Thoms scooped up the ball, ran 29 yards for a touchdown and we were ahead again. Then the Bills scored on another Ferguson-to-Rashad pass to go ahead, 21–20, with 26 seconds left. On the last play George Blanda tried a 50-yard field goal but missed. When you're a coach, that's the kind of see-saw game that stays with you. I was still steaming as I left the locker room for the chartered buses waiting to take us to the airport. On my way out, Howard Cosell was walking toward his limo.

"John," he said happily, "you gave us a great show."

"Show!" I roared. "A great show! To you it's a show but to me it's a goddam game we just lost! And there's nothing great about it! I don't think I've ever been so pissed off!"

Howard disappeared into his limo. I kept going and never looked back.

When you're involved in football as a coach—as I was for so long—a game is not a show. Anytime I hear a TV announcer talk about the "top of the show," it bothers me. "Laverne and Shirley"—that's a show. But a football game doesn't have a script—nobody knows what's going to happen. That's why so many people watch. Because it's a game, a competitive contest. Even now, working for CBS, a football game to me is always a game. Not a show.

In a sense, that's why I stopped coaching after the 1978 season. As the Raiders' coach, I had won every game there was to win.

As soon as we won Super Bowl XI after the 1976 season, I started thinking that I wouldn't go on coaching too much longer. I had only one more ambition— to win one hundred games my first ten years. After the 1977 season, when I had 94 regular-season victories, I realized that no coach in the NFL or the AFL had ever done that, especially with the same team.

"I've got a chance," I told my wife Virginia, "to do what no other coach has ever done."

As it developed, I won 103. (Virginia gave me a huge gold ring with "100" in diamonds on it.) But during that final 1978 season, I began to burn out. At the time I didn't think of it that way. Nobody was talking about "coaching burnout" then. I still don't like the phrase. It's too negative, too much of a catchall. But whatever you want to call it, I got to the point where I couldn't coach anymore. All my life, I've pictured myself doing things. Playing ball as a kid. Coaching on the sideline. Even now, in preparing for my TV games, I picture the players I'm going to be talking about. But in 1978, suddenly I couldn't picture myself on the sideline the next year. That's when I knew I'd had it. At our spring minicamp that year, I also had pains in my stomach that didn't go away. Even when I took a Rolaids or had a Pepto-Bismol, the pains didn't disappear. I asked our team physician, Dr. Don Fink, to check me out.

"You've got an ulcer," he told me. "Not a bleeding ulcer, just an ulcer. The only thing that will heal it is if you stop what's causing it—coaching. But this should control it. Take this four times a day."

He prescribed a pill that dried up the acid in my stomach, the acid from the coaching grind. By itself, the ulcer didn't persuade me to stop coaching. Lots of people work with ulcers. I could've kept coaching with it, but I just didn't *want* to keep coaching. It seemed like I never had a chance to recharge my batteries, especially after we won Super Bowl XI—I never had time to enjoy it. As soon as we got back from that Super Bowl, we started thinking about the college draft and our minicamp and then training camp and, boom, the season was starting. It seemed like we went from the Super Bowl to training camp without any break. Without any time off for myself or my family. So there I was, thinking about getting out with one hundred wins in ten years and taking pills for my ulcer when something else happened. Something really terrible.

Darryl Stingley, a wide receiver for the New Eng-

3

land Patriots, collided with Jack Tatum, our free safety, in an August 12th exhibition game in Oakland.

On the play, Darryl lined up as the Patriots' wide receiver on the right side at our 24-yard line. He ran downfield about 8 yards, then he slanted toward the middle to catch a pass from Steve Grogan, the Patriots' quarterback. But the ball was thrown a little too high. Darryl leaped for it, but the ball sailed past his fingers. Just then Jack Tatum crashed into him. Darryl sagged to the ground.

Darryl didn't move. Not a finger, not a foot. He still hadn't moved when a stretcher was wheeled out to take him into the locker room.

I'd gone through this once before. Back in 1972 one of our rookie running backs, Ray Jamieson from Memphis State, suffered a broken neck while making a tackle on a punt-return. He never played football again. He's able to walk now, but he's not able to work. (He's married with two boys and lives in Tennessee on disability payments from the NFL benefits plan.) I was thinking of Ray as Darryl was wheeled off, then went back to finishing the game. It wasn't until I was in our locker room that I heard Darryl was paralyzed with a broken neck.

"Where'd they take him?" I asked.

"Eden Hospital in Castro Valley."

On the field, we play hard. But when somebody on the other team gets hurt as seriously as Darryl did, we're all in this game together. By the time I got to the hospital, Darryl was being prepared for a "halo," a steel ring attached to an eighty-pound weight to keep a person's head immobile. Outside the operating room, I saw Dr. Don Fink.

"I want to see," I told him.

"You can't go in there that way," Don said, staring at my regular clothes. "Only doctors and nurses are allowed in there."

"Then get me one of those doctor's things."

He got me the biggest surgeon's smock he could find. Inside the operating room, Darryl was conscious. I bent down near him.

"Everything's going to be all right," I whispered. "Everything's going to be all right."

But everything didn't turn out to be all right. Darryl remains in a wheelchair, a quadriplegic. In my decision to stop coaching, Darryl's situation was a factor. Not the only factor, but *a* factor. During the weeks he was in Eden Hospital, not many people seemed to care enough. That's when I started wondering if football people really care about a player, or if football people just care about what a player does. And when a player suddenly can't do what he does, if football people don't care about him then, they probably never really cared about him to begin with.

As a coach, I might've been guilty of that too.

If I lost a linebacker for the season, I'm sure I told Al Davis, my boss on the Raiders, "I need a linebacker." It's like going to your auto mechanic and saying, "I need a battery." Coaches tend to talk about players that way, as if they were made out of metal instead of flesh and blood. Even worse, as if they were just a "body" instead of a person. But that Saturday night in 1978, a person had been paralyzed. And to me, not enough people seemed to care.

After Darryl's wife Tina arrived the next day, Virginia invited her to stay with us in Pleasanton, southeast of Oakland. Tina preferred to sleep in a hospital office near Darryl's room. But every so often she came over for dinner, talked with Virginia and our two sons, Mike and Joe, and watched television. Anything to take her mind off Darryl for a few hours. One afternoon Tina played one-on-one basketball with Mike on our backyard court, and she won.

"I learned all my moves," she said, "from Darryl."

I was busy coaching the Raiders, but whenever Virginia and I had the chance, we visited Darryl in the hospital. Some of the Raider players also visited him, but Darryl was bitter that Jack Tatum never came. Jack had tried. The day Jack arrived at the hospital, he was told he couldn't see Darryl. That wasn't unusual—whenever Darryl was being treated, nobody could see him. But I think Jack got the impression that Darryl didn't want to see him, or that Darryl's wife or his mother and brother didn't want Darryl to see him. Whatever it was, Jack left the hospital and never returned.

Looking back, I can see that I should have brought Jack in to see Darryl myself. Two months after the accident, it was too late. Darryl was flown to another hospital in Chicago, his hometown.

Darryl holds Jack responsible for what happened. But, watching their collision as it was happening, I didn't think Jack had hit Darryl any harder than he had hit some other receivers—maybe even not as hard. Watching the films later, the big thing to me was that Darryl got hit in mid-air. If one or both of his feet had been on the ground, he might have been able to absorb the hit. After it happened, nobody ever felt any worse about it than Jack did. I'm sure it'll always be on his mind.

Jack's part in the accident has been misunderstood. He was just doing what he had always done, what he had been coached to do, what he did as well as anybody in the NFL—hit hard.

In high school, coaches told him to hit hard, so he hit hard. At Ohio State, he was All-America because he hit hard. In the NFL, he was on three Pro Bowl teams because he hit hard. But after the accident, Jack Tatum was suddenly an evil player because he hit hard. Hell, that's why we drafted him—*because he hit hard*. On a Saturday during the 1970 season, I was watching an Ohio State game on television when Jack made three of the damndest tackles I'd ever seen.

"That kid really hits," I remember saying. "I'd love to have him."

When it was our turn in the first round of the 1971 draft, Jack was available. He was a great player for the Raiders; not just a good player, a great player. Then he put Darryl Stingley into a wheelchair for life, prompting some people to complain that the NFL is too violent. It probably is, but other than abolishing the game, I don't know what you can do to make it less violent. Players are bigger, stronger, and faster than ever. When you get two big strong guys running into each other, that's a violent act. Down on the field, it even *sounds* violent. When players collide with all that equipment on, it sounds like a car wreck. Violence often is confused with dirty football, but some of the most violent acts in football are within the rules. Jack Tatum, for example, wasn't penalized when he hit Darryl Stingley, nor should he have been.

When the 1978 season ended and we missed the playoffs, I was ready to retire. I had had one hundred and three wins in ten years. I had my Super Bowl ring. I had my ulcer. And for several months following Darryl's accident, I had thought it all over.

I hadn't told anybody about my plan to retire except Virginia and our boys. I knew they would keep my secret. I also knew that if I had confided in anybody on the club, it would get out somehow—and I didn't want it to. I didn't want the team laboring under a lame-duck coach. I didn't want Al Davis and the other coaches and the players constantly being asked about next year. I just kept coaching. And not very well. We lost three in a row before finishing with a 27–20 win over the Vikings at Oakland, but until I got home that night, it hadn't occurred to me that it had been my last game. I waited a week. Then the day after Christmas, a Tuesday morning, I walked into Al's office and sat down.

"The way I feel now, I've had it," I said. "You better start thinking about a new coach."

Al knew I hadn't been myself all season, but he had no inkling that I was thinking of not coaching anymore.

"Are you sure?" he asked.

"I'm pretty sure," I said.

"Take some time to think it over," he suggested. "Take a vacation. If you still feel that way, let me know."

I agreed. "I'll let you know next week."

Virginia and I had been invited to spend New Year's Eve in Las Vegas, so we drove over there and laughed at Don Rickles' insults. But the more I thought about coaching, the more I couldn't picture myself doing it anymore. On the drive home, we were in a roadside restaurant having dinner when I decided to phone Al.

"I'm sure," I announced.

"You're really sure?" Al asked.

"I'm positive."

"Well, we've got to announce that, John, but I want you to stay in the organization."

"As long as it has nothing to do with football."

The morning after we got home, I talked with Al and he put me in charge of "special projects"—whatever that means. I'm still listed on the Raiders' administrative staff with that title. At my press conference on January 4, 1979, exactly ten years to the day from when I was named the Raiders' coach, I talked about how I had done everything a coach could do and about how I just didn't want to do it anymore.

"I want to be with my family," I said.

I told about the time Virginia mentioned to me that I should start thinking about buying a car for Mike.

"He's got a few years," I told her.

"What do you mean, he's got a few years?" she said. "He's old enough for his driver's permit. He's sixteen."

I'd thought he was twelve.

My intentions were good. I really wanted to spend more time with Virginia and the boys. Except it turned out they couldn't spend that much time with me. Virginia had learned to do things on her own. At training camp one year, I kept phoning home day after day without getting an answer. At first, I figured I had called when everybody happened to be out. After a few more days, I was starting to get worried, but that night Virginia answered.

"We were away," she explained. "I took the kids down to Mexico for a few days."

Once you give somebody that much rope, you can't suddenly pull it back. By now, Virginia was busy with a little wine-and-beer bar she owned over in Dublin near where we live. After school, our boys were busy with their sports or their friends. So I found myself watching TV soap operas and talking to our English bulldog, Boss. By then I discovered that the real-estate business with my friend Jim Lange wasn't enough to keep me busy. My first day there, I sat around the office drinking coffee, had lunch, and then stood on line at City Hall to get a sewer permit for a shopping mall. I wasn't sure what I wanted to do with the rest of my life, but I sure as hell knew I didn't want to spend it getting sewer permits.

After that, I decided not to do anything. I had some real-estate investments. I had enough income to hold me. Then one day the phone rang.

Barry Frank, the president of Trans World International, was wondering if I'd be interested in working for CBS as a TV analyst on their NFL games. TWI handles television and radio for the International Management Group, which Mark McCormack started as Arnold Palmer's attorney. At the Super Teams competition between the Super Bowl champions and the World Series champions in Hawaii early in 1977, Mark had talked about representing me in business opportunities outside football. But as far as I was concerned then, there was nothing for them to represent. I was a football coach, period.

"I'm not the type of guy who's ever going to have a TV show or a radio show," I told Ira Miller of the *San Francisco Chronicle* shortly before I stopped coaching. "I'm not the type of guy who's ever going to do a book."

I've done all three now—TV for CBS, a radio show five times a week for RKO, and you're reading the book. At the time, though, I never dreamed of doing any of these things. The day Barry Frank phoned, I wasn't interested in doing anything, much less television. If you retire from one job and go to work the next day at another, you're probably just running from that first job, which I wasn't.

"But it's just a part-time deal," Barry told me. "Five or six games for CBS next season."

"Yeah, but I don't know if I want to do that. I really don't want to do anything."

"You ought to try it, John," he said. "If you try it and you don't like it, at least you tried it, at least you know you don't like it. But if you wait two or three years and then decide you want to try it, the networks will have forgotten about you."

"Yeah, that's a good point," I had to admit.

As soon as Barry began talking about two or three years down the road, I remembered what I had always told our rookies in training camp. "At one time or another," I said, "each and every one of you is going to think about leaving here. Believe me, whether you're our first-round choice or the last free agent we signed, you'll think about going home. But when you start thinking about leaving, don't worry about it. Everybody thinks about it. Just remember that if you do leave and in another two or three years you want to come back, it'll be too late." Talking on the phone now with Barry Frank about CBS being interested in me, I thought about what I had told my rookies.

"Barry, you're right," I said. "I'll try it."

2

Just Be Yourself

ALL MY LIFE, I'VE BEEN BIG ON PREPARATION. As a coach, I prepared game plans, I prepared for the college draft. As a player, I prepared for games, for practices. As a student and as a teacher, I prepared for class. As soon as I signed my CBS contract in 1979, I naturally wanted to learn how to prepare to be a TV game analyst.

"Don't worry," CBS people kept telling me. "Just be yourself."

Be yourself? What's that supposed to mean? Everybody has a lot of different selves. Did that mean be funny? Be serious? Be brief? Be long? Be basic? Be technical?

"Don't worry," CBS people kept telling me. "Just come to the seminar."

Yeah, the seminar. I really learned a lot at the seminar. I learned that New York in June is hot as hell. I learned that the big glass-and-concrete CBS building on West 52nd Street had a nickname—Black Rock, because it's black. I learned how to make out a CBS expense account. At least I thought I did. Halfway through my first season, I was informed that I had to itemize all my expenses for travel, hotel, and meals. (I had thought they were automatically billed to CBS through my credit card.) But at the seminar, I had another question.

"Now that I'm an announcer," I kept asking, "what do I do?"

"Just talk to the people out there. Just talk football."

"But what people am I talking to out there? To grownups? To kids? To guys? To gals? To players? To ex-players? To people who know football? To people who don't know anything at all about football?"

"To all of 'em."

I guess the CBS people could tell that I seemed to be groping, which I definitely was. To make things worse, I had nothing to take back to California to study. No notebooks, no instruction manual, no nothing. About all I had was a promise that I would "practice" doing a game before I really did one. That sounded good, but I was still groping. I even decided to go to one of the Raiders' exhibition games to practice myself. But when I got there, I felt lost. All those years as a coach, I knew where to go in the Oakland Coliseum and what I was supposed to do. But now that I was there by myself, I didn't know where to go or even where to sit.

"How come you're home so early?" Virginia asked.

"I just left," I told her. "I didn't know what to do."

My practice game would be the San Francisco 49ers against the Rams in the Los Angeles Coliseum, the third Sunday of the 1979 season. Vince Scully and

George Allen were really doing that game, but CBS put me in another booth with Bob Costas as my play-by-play announcer. Bob and I had headsets connected to Tom O'Neil, our director. Our monitors were showing the same picture that Vin and George were watching. We couldn't hear what they were saying, but I didn't want to hear them. I was too busy practicing my own commentary.

As it turned out, my biggest problem that day was that I had stayed down on the field too long before the game.

I had gone down there to practice a taped opening. But then I had to go back outside the Coliseum, wait my turn to get into the elevator and then find our TV booth. Once there, I realized I hadn't left myself enough time to adjust to watching a game from up there. In the L.A. Coliseum the TV-radio booths are not only among the highest in the NFL but also the furthest back from the field itself. As soon as I looked down from the booth, I knew I had to learn to watch football all over again. On the sideline I knew what all twenty-two players did on every play. But from up in that booth at the L.A. Coliseum, the players looked smaller than they do on game films. I gradually adjusted to that sightline, but it took time.

I did my first real "live" game the following Sunday, the 49ers against the New Orleans Saints at Candlestick Park. This time I got up to the booth early and checked out the sightline and my headset. Frank Glieber was my play-by-play announcer. Duke Struck was my director (in TV, a director selects what pictures to use from all the different cameras he's got). Tom O'Neil, who had been my director for my "practice" game, now was my producer (a producer organizes and supervises the telecast). During the first half I was watching the monitor in our booth when a shot appeared of Bill Walsh on the sideline. I suddenly heard Tom's voice in my headset.

"Coach, coach," he was saying.

"Yeah, what do you want?" I said without thinking. "What do you want?"

"No, no," I heard. "*That* coach."

Tom had wanted me to talk about Bill Walsh, the 49ers' coach whose picture was on the screen. But through all my years as a coach, so many people had addressed me as "coach," when I heard Tom calling, "coach, coach," I thought he meant me. Getting used to the voice of the producer or the director in your headset takes a little time. The trick is, you're supposed to listen to what they're saying, but not answer. Near the end of the first half in that first game, I suddenly had another problem.

"It looks like we won't be able to synch up with New York at halftime," Tom said. "We'll have to do our own halftime."

Synch up with New York—what was that supposed to mean? I learned later that if your halftime intermission arrives around the same time as that of the other games in that time slot, the announcers can relax while "The NFL Today" show fills those fifteen minutes. But if your first half is slow and doesn't end until well after "The NFL Today" has taken over at halftime of the other games—in other words, if your game isn't synchronized or in "synch" with the other games, the announcers must supply the halftime show.

"We didn't synch up, we've got to do our own halftime," I heard Tom say now. "John, I want you to interview Dan Abramowicz; he should be right there behind you in the booth."

I looked around and there he was, my halftime guest, as if by magic—Dan Abramowicz, the former wide receiver with the Saints and 49ers who had become a color commentator on the Saints' radio broadcasts.

"It's halftime," Frank Glieber was saying now, "and John Madden will be interviewing Dan Abramowicz . . . John?"

During that introduction, I was thinking that while I had done TV interviews for years, I always had been the interviewee, not the interviewer. I always answered questions, never asked them. In trying to think of a question for Dan, it occurred to me that Frank and I had been talking about how we had thought before the game that the 49ers would throw a lot and the Saints would run a lot but that just the opposite had happened.

"Thanks for coming by, Dan, it's nice to see you again," I said. "It's been a strange first half—the 49ers have passed more than I thought they would and the Saints have run more than I thought they would."

I put the microphone in front of Dan, who stared at me for a moment. I hadn't asked a question. I simply had made a statement. When he realized that I had said all I was going to say, he started talking. With his help, I got through the interview. But if Dan had kept staring at me after my opening statement, I don't know what might have happened. After that, whenever I had to interview somebody, I tried to prepare some questions.

But when that first game was over, I knew being a TV analyst was what I wanted to do.

I remembered Bear Bryant once saying, "Don't be

a football coach unless you can't live without it." That's why I had been a football coach—I couldn't live without it, at least not until after I'd been the Raiders' coach for ten years. Since I stopped coaching, several NFL and USFL teams have asked if I was interested in being a coach again. I'm not. I tell them no, and I mean no. I don't mean that I want more money. As a TV analyst, I still have a football season. I think that's what most guys miss when they leave the sport. From the time you're a kid, your life has been built around a season. As soon as you don't have that season, every day is the same, every week is the same. Even worse, every Sunday is the same. I now have the best possible football season.

For me, TV is really an extension of coaching. My knowledge of football has come from coaching. And on TV, all I'm trying to do is pass on some of that knowledge to the viewers.

One of my tests for a good telecast is if I didn't miss anything. If the coaches or players later mention something significant about the game that I didn't mention, I'm not happy. Another test is whether I feel the viewer has learned something about football or football people. Women viewers too. Almost all the women I've ever talked to about football have wanted to learn the game because of their husband or their boyfriend or their sons. I'd like to see women learn to appreciate football for themselves, not just for the males in their lives. Helping the viewer—male or female—to learn is why we developed the "Chalkboard" on our CBS telecasts. Several months before the 1981 season, I was having dinner one night with Terry O'Neil, the CBS Sports executive producer for NFL games.

"John," he said, "you should have a special coach's camera with all twenty-two players in the picture."

"That's what coaching film looks like," I said. "That's what I've always wanted to have."

On your TV set, when the teams line up for a play, you usually see most of the offense, but seldom all of the defense. You never see what all twenty-two players are doing on each play. If your set showed a wide enough picture to see all of the players, they would appear too small for most viewers to follow. But from that conversation we developed the Chalkboard, which enables me to diagram how a play develops. For me, it's like being a teacher again at Hancock Junior College, San Diego State, or at the University of California at Berkeley where I held two-day seminars on "Man to Man Football" after I stopped coaching. To the viewer, the Chalkboard is simply a visual aid that makes it easier to understand what's happening. Football isn't nuclear physics, but it's not so simple that you can make it simple. It takes some explaining to get it across.

In the TV booth, I'm the same guy I was as a coach on the sideline. Most announcers sit down, but I prefer to stand up, to swing my arms, to move around as much as possible. I once knocked Gary Bender's glasses off. Just before the game and at halftime, you see me with my tie on straight and wearing a blue blazer. CBS rules. But when I'm not on camera, my tie is loose and I'm in shirtsleeves, just like I was on the sideline. For me to do it any other way wouldn't be natural. And on TV, you have to be natural or you come across as a phoney.

For that reason, I don't watch video-tapes of my games. If you critique yourself, you're going to change some things. If you change too much, suddenly you're no longer natural.

Going into a game, I want to know as much as I can about a team, about its coach, about its players, about its plans. My first year as an analyst, I noticed that some CBS people thought that having a drink with a team's public-relations man passed for research. But that wasn't enough for me.

The day before a game, we try to attend each team's practice. Then we talk to some of the players and sit down with each coach for at least an hour. I'm not looking for any secret plays—I'm just trying to pick up information I can pass on to the viewers. But when we talked to Bill Parcells, the Giants' coach, the day before his 1983 season opener against the Rams, he sounded a little hesitant in his answers.

"I'm a little scared about telling you all this," he finally said. "I know you're a good friend of John Robinson." (John Robinson, the Rams' new coach that year, and I had grown up together in Daly City outside San Francisco.)

"I guarantee you, Bill, that I'm not going to tell another coach what you say any more than I'm going to tell you what another coach says. The first time I ever do that with any coach, I'm through."

I was a little annoyed that Bill would even think I might do that, but at the time he was a rookie coach awaiting his first NFL game. He soon loosened up. As we talked, he told me about how his rookie place-kicker, Ali Haji-Sheikh, pulled a leg muscle early in training camp. At first the Giants feared Ali would be out six weeks.

"The next day when I went out to my car after practice, Ali was sitting in it," Bill said. "He looked at me and told me, 'I'll be ready in three days.' Not quite. But he was ready in six."

That's the type of story I'm looking for when I talk to a coach, not for a trick play he plans to use. The type of story a viewer can relate to—a rookie who doesn't want to lose his chance for a job. As it turned out, Ali Haji-Sheikh was the consensus All-Pro place-kicker as a rookie. Looking back now, it was fun for me to tell the viewers that story about him during his very first game.

I once almost had another story to tell about a kicker, an embarrassing story.

The day before a game in Dallas, I was watching the Cowboys practice when Rafael Septien tossed me a football. I tossed it back. Kickers just stand around during practice anyway, so pretty soon we were playing catch the way kids do—leading the other guy, making him run to catch your pass. After a few passes, I led Rafael too much. Right into a big lineman. Whoom, he went down in a heap. He got up, but a little slowly. I looked around to see if Tom Landry or any of the other Cowboy coaches had noticed. It didn't look like they had but I got the hell out of there.

After practice, I looked up to see Rafael coming toward me, limping, with an Ace bandage on the knee of his kicking foot. I thought, *oh no,* but it was just a gag. Rafael was just having some fun.

I'm always asked if TV is more fun for me than coaching was, but those people don't understand that it doesn't have to be more fun. As a coach, I enjoyed the big games the most, but I also enjoyed my players, training camp, practices, watching films, working with the other coaches, working with Al Davis and the office staff—everything. I never got to the point where I didn't enjoy football, because I stopped coaching when I realized I was approaching that point. But as soon as I started doing TV, I enjoyed it too. Coaching *was* fun, but now TV *is* fun. Except for Christmas week.

The first time I had to do an NFL playoff game in Christmas week was 1980—the Cowboys against the Rams at Texas Stadium.

When I travel, I don't fly. I ride trains. I couldn't be home in Pleasanton with Virginia and the boys for Christmas on Thursday and still get to Dallas in time for Sunday's game, so I invited them to spend Christmas with me at the Hyatt Regency in Dallas.

I got a big suite. I even had a decorated Christmas tree brought up, sort of a room-service Christmas tree.

But the hotel was empty, the downtown area was empty, my Christmas spirit was empty. Everybody else was home for Christmas, which is where everybody is supposed to be. Everybody but me and my wife and our boys. The worst was Christmas Eve. I made reservations for Christmas Eve dinner at the Reunion Tower restaurant with a revolving floor built on stilts atop the equivalent of a fifty-two-floor office building. With my dislike for heights, I should have known better. As bad as I felt on the elevator ride up, I felt worse when I stepped out onto a floor that was moving. Moving very slowly, but nevertheless moving. After we were ushered to a table overlooking downtown Dallas, I sat there for a few moments, then bolted out of my chair.

"I can't eat here," I said.

Virginia and the boys understood, but I told them to stay. No use spoiling their dinner. I went back and had dinner in the Hyatt Regency coffee shop, the only person in there. Maybe it's me, but I've never been in a restaurant that's on top of a building—or even just off the ground—that was any good. Virginia and the boys tried to pretend they were having a good time on that Christmas trip. But they weren't and neither was I. Never again.

The way the NFL schedule works, I've always had a game at Christmas. But I've never asked my family to join me again. Being away at Christmas is my problem, not theirs.

As the extra analyst in 1979, my first season at CBS, I only worked when there were enough games for the network to need me. I teamed with Pat Summerall, Dick Stockton and Lindsay Nelson in addition to Frank Glieber, which was great experience. I had to adjust to each announcer's style. I also was working with a number of producers and directors. This way I didn't learn just one way to do it, but a lot of different ways.

I also learned all those players' names and numbers which my Pleasanton neighbor, Carl Marsh, puts on the big Spotters Board he makes up for me for each game.

But by watching films and by looking at both teams practice the day before a game, I learned to identify many players from their body movements or from the way their body looks in a uniform. As the Raiders' coach, I never had to look at any of my players' numbers to know who he was. I knew from the way he ran or the way he moved. I knew most of the opposing players too, especially those who had been around the NFL for a few years. Up in my TV booth, I wanted to be able to identify as many players as possible—without looking at a number. Of course, in a pileup it doesn't make much difference. To make sure, I always wait until they unpile—unless it's a Cowboy pileup. Once,

I turned to Pat Summerall as we watched the players getting up from a goal-line pileup.

"That little number helps," I said.

"What little number?" Pat asked.

"See that little number on the Cowboys' pants?" I said, referring to a new small number the Cowboys had put hip high on both sides of their players' silver pants. "That really helps in a pileup."

"So it does," agreed Pat.

Pat Summerall is as easy to work with as he is to be with. He's easy to hang out with, to tell stories with, and I think that comes across to the viewer. He's just a good guy. He has things I don't, but I don't think I have anything he doesn't. I like to bluster about a play, but Pat will sum it up in a few words. One time I was raving about a great catch a wide receiver had made, about how he had juggled the ball like an acrobat before finally hanging onto it.

"That guy," Pat commented, "should've been a waiter."

As simple as that. As quick as that. As good as that. Pat and I have been working together now since the 1981 season. Most of that time we've had Bob Stenner as producer and Sandy Grossman as director. Pat helped me learn how to talk about what Sandy was putting on the screen. That wasn't always what I wanted to talk about, but that's TV—you talk about what's on the screen, about what the viewers are seeing.

From the beginning of my CBS career, I've watched the Monday night game and any other game as often as possible. Watching another person doing a game, I'm always thinking about what I would be saying if I were doing it. You can take certain things lightly, things even the coach or the players will be able to laugh about later. Like when two guards pull to block on a sweep and one guard runs the wrong way— smack into the other guard. When the coach and the players see that on the game films, they'll laugh harder than the viewers did during the game. But if a coach makes a decision that doesn't work, that's not funny. If a receiver drops a pass in the clear, that's not funny.

To the TV executives, football is a TV show. But to the fans, it's a game, a serious game. And to the coaches and the players, it's a livelihood. I'd never make fun of somebody's livelihood.

But in the TV booth I like to have some fun. I've often said, "I've never met a great player who wasn't a little goofy." I think people know I mean "goofy" to be a positive quality. It's like saying that a genius is a little whacky—that's what makes a genius. And being a little goofy is what makes a player great. I had some other lines that also appealed to people: "His light is on, but there's nobody home." "His elevator doesn't go all the way to the top." "One knee equals two feet."

Around that time I was invited to host "Saturday Night Live," which scared the hell out of me. I'd never done anything like that. To find out if I should start preparing anything or rehearsing some lines, I phoned Dick Ebersol, the show's executive producer.

"No," he said, "just be here in my office the Tuesday morning after the Super Bowl."

I expected him to hand me a script when I walked in. But that early in the week there's no script, no sets, no nothing. I wondered what crazy stuff he might want me to do, but he put me at ease about that.

"We don't want you to do anything," he said, "that you think would make you look bad."

On that show, I had figured I might be asked to do

almost anything, so that sounded nice. Then he stared at me, sizing me up.

"How," he said, "would you like to be a circus elephant?"

"You just told me I wouldn't have to do anything stupid."

"This is a retired circus elephant," Dick said. "He's living in a house with somebody taking care of him."

"I'd rather not," I said.

"No problem," Dick said.

After a while, some of the actors and writers joined us. They bounced around some ideas. One was to do a takeoff on "Up With People," the Super Bowl halftime show that year.

"Let's do 'Down With People,'" somebody suggested.

They talked about how only the players in the winning team's locker room were interviewed on TV after the Super Bowl.

"Let's do the losing team's locker room," another person in the group said.

Whoever suggested an idea, wrote the scene. All through the discussion, I just sat there. Finally I looked over to Dick.

"But what do *I* do?" I said.

"We'll think of something."

That was the most fun about being on "Saturday Night Live"—starting with nothing and building something. By Wednesday some of the show was written. Thursday, you went into a studio with a rough script. Friday, you went into the studio again. But as late as Saturday afternoon, the show was still being written and rewritten. Nobody was completely sure, not even Dick, what was going to be in the show and what wasn't. I never talked to Dick about this approach to putting on a TV show, but that's the way I was as a coach. I always believed that if you got your complete game plan done too early, what would you do between that time and the time you've got left? One thing you do is get bored. If you're under the gun, however, you're working until the last minute. But after a dress rehearsal at 7:30 on Saturday evening, I thought I knew what the show was going to be like—until Dick walked into my dressing room.

"We're changing the order," he said.

At the dress rehearsal, some scenes had gotten bigger laughs than others, so Dick put all those laughs up front. Half an hour before we went on, I was handed the new order of scenes. That wasn't much time for me to learn the new order and the new wardrobe changes. After wearing a sweater in a bar scene, I had to rush to a poetry-reading scene where I would wear a smoking jacket. Hurrying backstage, I saw the wardrobe man holding out my smoking jacket. I stuck an arm in a sleeve.

"No, no, no, take the sweater off," he said. "Take it off."

"I don't have time," I said, putting on the smoking jacket.

I got to my chair in the poetry corner just in time. But as far as TV goes, my elevator "doesn't go all the way to the top." If anything, it's stuck between floors. I'm not really part of that world. For instance, I don't know the inner workings of actual TV production. I don't know what goes on in those meetings at the CBS building because I'm seldom there. I don't have an office or a secretary. I don't even have a desk or a telephone. I make my own train reservations. Our home is still in Pleasanton, but when I'm in New York Virginia and I stay in the city at our apartment on the Upper West Side across from Central Park.

When Virginia and I were deciding on where to live around New York, we first looked at houses in Connecticut. But in California our home is in a suburb, so for a change we started to look for a place in Manhattan. We checked out some solidly built lofts in SoHo but the people down there weren't my kind of people. Neither were the people on the East Side—too formal. When we looked on the West Side, we both felt more comfortable.

Our New York apartment building is one hundred years old, a big, brown-brick, nine-story fortress with a cement courtyard in the middle. Once you're inside your apartment, you don't hear any of the city noises. No traffic, no horns, no nothing. Some celebrities live there but I prefer to hang out with Joe the doorman and José in the office and just stand around watching people come and go. Our first Halloween there, I saw a guy coming out of Central Park in a crazy getup.

"Hey, that's a good Halloween costume," I said.

"That's not a costume," Joe replied. "That guy looks like that every day."

"Oh," I said.

That night I saw a guy in a baby-blue ballerina's tutu with baby-blue tights. I *think* it was a costume. But hey, living in an apartment is great. When it snows, I don't have to shovel it. When something goes wrong, I don't have to fix it. (In fact, Virginia really likes that more than I do. In our family, she's the one with a tool kit, not me.) The building is so nice, I wonder sometimes how I got in. Especially after I settled my 270 pounds onto an antique wooden straight-back chair in the apartment of Richard Lukins, one of the building's directors. Every time I shifted my weight, the chair creaked. And when I crossed my legs, it creaked a little louder. Mr. Lukins finally looked over at me from the big soft chair he was sitting in.

"Why don't you sit here?" he offered.

"No, no, I'm fine," I said. "I'm fine."

"I know *you're* fine," he said, "but you're going to break my chair. Please sit in this chair."

We switched chairs. It's probably just as well. Our meeting lasted nearly two hours, and I don't know if that antique chair would have lasted that long with me on it. Wearing a tie and jacket that long, I almost didn't last, either. I'm not a dress-up guy. I mostly wear short-sleeved sportshirts, jeans and sneakers, with the laces untied.

One of the few times I wear a suit and tie in New York is for the annual Emmy Awards for Sports Programming, which are selected by the National Academy of TV Arts and Sciences. For the 1981 award in the Sports Personality, Analyst category, I had been nominated along with Billy Packer (for college basketball), Dave Marr (for golf), Nelson Burton, Jr. (for bowling), and Dick Button (for figure skating). I was hoping to win, but I didn't dare think about an acceptance speech. That would have been presumptuous. It would be like designing a Super Bowl ring before winning the game. But without a speech ready, I knew I'd sound like a dummy if I did win.

"The envelope, please," I heard Brent Musberger say. "And the winner is ... John Madden."

Music, applause, just like the Oscars awards for movie stars. I hurried up onto the stage where Brent handed me my Emmy—a gold winged lady atop a golden globe.

"Now I know," I began, "why nobody ever makes any sense when they win an award like this."

I explained that I hadn't prepared a speech because I didn't want to be presumptuous. And now that I hadn't prepared anything, I was sure I sounded like a dummy—just like I thought I would. I went on to thank Pat Summerall, all the producers and directors, all the CBS executives who had faith in me.

Then, for a switch, I decided to thank three guys nobody ever talks about, three guys I'd be lost without.

"They always work in three's," I said. "You're getting ready to do a game and you're testing your headset. 'Yeah, I hear you, Bob....' 'Yeah, I hear you, Sandy....' But a minute before air, suddenly nothing works. 'I can't hear you, Bob....' 'I can't hear you, Sandy....' As soon as that happens these three guys come running up out of nowhere."

I told the audience one guy always stinks with body odor. The other guy always has a cigar sticking out of his mouth and his glasses are falling off. The third guy's belly sticks out below his T-shirt and the top of his ass is sticking out above his jeans. They climb all over you and around you, step on your Spotters Board, spill your cup of coffee. But somehow—just in time—they fix your headset so you can hear voices again.

"That's how you start each game—with those same three guys who come out of nowhere and then disappear," I said. "In the booth, you never get a chance to talk to them, so I'd like to thank them now."

Again, just like at the Oscars. Giving a final wave, I left and walked to the side where a young lady approached me.

"I'll take your Emmy now, Mr. Madden," she said, reaching for the award I received only moments before. "We only have about a dozen here. You'll receive your actual Emmy in a few weeks."

"No, no, you're not taking this," I replied. "I'm taking it back to my table to show it to my friends. No, no, I'm keeping this. You can't take this away from me tonight."

"But you don't understand, Mr. Madden."

"I do understand. I just won an Emmy!"

I was just having some fun with her. I was going to return it to her later, but I guess she didn't realize that. Back at my table, I looked up to see her standing next to me.

"Mr. Madden," she said, "I really need that Emmy."

My very own Emmy was delivered a few weeks later. I also won an Emmy in 1982, again in the Analyst category against different competition—Merlin Olsen (for pro football), Frank Broyles (for college football), Joe Garagiola (for baseball), and Al McGuire (for college basketball). Whenever I'm asked to talk about my two Emmys, I just grunt.

"Huh?" I say.

I'm just being myself.

3

Set Up the House

I TRAVELED BY AIR ALL THE TIME I WAS COACHING, but I was never a good flyer. If the takeoff was smooth and the flight was smooth, I coped with it—but I never enjoyed it. As soon as the seat-belt sign flashed on for our landing, my stomach flashed on, too. Especially when there was cloud cover.

"See the ground yet?" I'd keep saying. "See any lights yet?"

As a coach, I had to go with the Raiders wherever they went, so I had to fly with them. On a charter, though, you're able to get up and walk around more than you can on a regular commercial flight. That relaxed me a little. But after I gave up coaching, I thought I'd slow down now that I had more time. I went by train to attend a football dinner in Milwaukee, then I took the train home. I later took the train all the way to New York and back with my boys to do my first Miller Lite commercial. But once I began working

NFL games for CBS, I was flying again. Not that I wanted to, but it saved time.

The morning of November 12, 1979, I was on a jetliner to San Francisco after having done a Packers–Vikings game in Milwaukee. As soon as we took off, I felt more woozy than usual. I broke into a cold sweat. My legs were weak. I glanced at the seat-belt sign, thinking maybe there was some turbulence I hadn't noticed. But the sign wasn't lit. The takeoff had been smooth. Now, as we were leveling off at about 35,000 feet and moving over the farmlands of Wisconsin and Iowa, the flight was still smooth, but I wasn't.

"What would you like to drink, sir?" I heard the flight attendant say.

"Nothing," I said. "Nothing to drink. Nothing to eat. Nothing at all."

I bolted out of my aisle seat and hurried to the rest room. Not to throw up. Just to be on my feet. I must have stayed in there half an hour, staring into the mirror at the cold sweat glistening on my forehead. After a while, I felt a little better. But as soon as I returned to my seat, the same wooziness came over me and the same cold sweat broke out. I got up and walked back and forth in the middle of the first-class cabin. But when some of the other passengers began to glance up at me, I disappeared into the rest room for the last two hours of the flight.

When we landed at San Francisco International and rolled up to the gate, I was the first passenger off.

The next morning, I went to see Dr. Don Fink, the Raiders' team physician, who is also my personal physician. He discovered that I had an infected ear that probably was aggravating the sinus condition I've had for years.

"Take these antibiotics," he told me as he wrote a prescription. "You should be all right in a few days."

I didn't have a game the following Sunday. After that I was scheduled to go to Tampa the Friday after Thanksgiving for a Bucs–Packers game Sunday afternoon. On the flight to Tampa, the same wooziness occurred, the same cold sweat. But this time I wasn't quite so concerned. I assumed that the antibiotics had not yet cleared up the ear infection. After the game, I boarded a return flight to San Francisco, with a stop in Houston.

I settled into my first-class seat, right side, on the aisle, across from the big door that was swung back while the passengers got on.

But as soon as the flight attendant slammed that door shut, I got woozy again. Worse than ever. That cold sweat and that weakness in my legs. I thought, *Jump up and open that door and get the hell off this plane*. And then I thought, *No, don't make an ass of yourself*. I was arguing with myself now—*get off, stay on . . . get off, stay on*. I stayed on. That two-hour flight to Houston was the most miserable experience of my life. I tried to walk the aisle. I tried standing in the rest room. Nothing helped.

In those two hours, I made up my mind that I was never going to fly again.

When we landed at the Houston Intercontinental Airport, I checked into a nearby motel and phoned Virginia to tell her what happened. As always, she understood.

"I'm taking the train to Los Angeles," I told her.

"I'll drive down there and pick you up," she said.

I didn't know at the time that I could have changed in Los Angeles to another train that would have taken me up to Oakland and saved her the trip to pick up me and my little briefcase. (My bags had been checked through to San Francisco, so they got home several days before I did.) But at the time I wasn't thinking about train routes or my luggage—only about my claustrophobia and what my alternatives were now. One, resign my job at CBS and find something else to do in the California area. Two, get medical help or seek professional counseling. Three, travel by train. I rejected the idea of leaving CBS because I was enjoying the work too much. I didn't want to take medicine in order to fly. I had enough problems when I was in complete control of myself. And when I realized that I could get anywhere in the NFL by train from one Sunday to the next, I didn't need professional counseling. My decision was obvious. Amtrak's timetable was my new playbook. But now I had a new problem. I was too embarrassed to tell the people at CBS or Miller Lite that I preferred to travel by train.

"I'll make my own arrangements," I'd say.

"We'll pick you up at the airport when you arrive," somebody would tell me. "What flight will you be on?"

"Don't bother picking me up. I'll be all right."

When it was time for a CBS production meeting or a Miller Lite taping, I would walk in on time.

"How was your flight?" somebody would ask.

"I had a good trip," I'd say. "Good trip."

That way I wasn't lying. Not that anybody was paying attention. But one day somebody from CBS phoned me at home.

"John left yesterday," Virginia said.

"I thought he was taking a flight tomorrow," the voice at CBS said.

"No, he left yesterday," she said.

"Then he must be in New York now."

"Well, no, he's not there yet."

"Did he stop somewhere on the way?"

"I guess he did," she said vaguely.

After a while people started to wonder why it took me three days to fly to New York, so I decided to tell all. I quickly found out that I never should have been embarrassed. Many people who fly told me they would prefer to take the train, but their tight schedule of business commitments doesn't permit them. When a few articles about my train travels appeared in newspapers and magazines, some people told me they realized the train could be an alternative for them.

I probably travel more miles by train than anybody else in America. I do about one hundred thousand miles a year. I know the timetables. I know the trains by their numbers as well as their names. For example, even-numbered trains go east and north, odd-numbered trains go west and south. As easy as that might sound, I could never remember which was which until a conductor set me straight. "Just remember," he said, "that the odds go to San Francisco." After that, I never had any trouble remembering.

The train is the closest I've come to fulfilling my fantasy of seeing America as John Steinbeck did in his book, *Travels with Charley*, with his dog. Like the Amtrak ads say, you really do see America—the mountains, the desert, the prairies, the farmland, the little towns, the big cities. What's even more fun, you see the people. Sitting in the club car for a few hours, I might talk with a dozen people, maybe two dozen. You don't do that on a plane. Most passengers on a plane never even talk to the person in the next seat. On a train, especially in a club car, it's different. If you don't start a conversation, somebody else will. One time we were coming out of Los Angeles on the way to Dallas when Andy appeared in the club car. I knew his name was Andy because the back of his thick leather belt had "Andy" tooled into it. Believe me, he was a perfect Andy—blue shirt, tan Bermuda shorts, black socks, black shoes, gray-haired, about sixty years old, a little heavy.

"First beer I've had in a week," he announced. "Been staying with a minister, he wouldn't let me drink."

Just then the conductor walked by. Andy asked him where and when we stopped in Arizona and New Mexico.

"I've set foot in forty-six states," he told the conductor, "and when I set foot in Arizona and New Mexico, I'll have set foot in all forty-eight—yes, sir, all forty-eight."

The conductor looked at me and I looked away. Neither of us had the heart to tell him there were fifty states now.

"Yes, sir," Andy repeated, gulping his beer, "not many people have set foot in all forty-eight. Yes, sir, not many."

In the lounge car the next day, Andy was still crowing about setting foot in all forty-eight states when a doctor across the aisle spoke up.

"But there are fifty states, Andy," he said.

"Not to me," Andy said. "Only forty-eight count."

By now, I've been on trains in most of those forty-eight states. One time in Montana, on the way to Seattle, a freight train ahead of us derailed. When we stopped in Culbertson, I walked down the main street of this little dusty town with a saloon right out of a John Wayne movie. I walked in and pounded a fist on the bar.

"Set up the house," I said, "I'm buying!"

The bartender looked at me strangely but started pouring drinks for the half-dozen townspeople sitting around.

"I've always wanted to do this," I said, laughing. "Set up the house."

To those people, a Miller Lite commercial had come to life. And no one enjoyed it any more than I did. Well, maybe the one-legged guy at the end of the bar did. He had been sitting with a woman who was just having coffee. But when he heard me buying drinks, he hobbled out on his crutch and took the woman with him. In a few minutes, he hobbled back in, this time with another guy. He sat down again at the end of the bar, then turned to his friend and pointed at me.

"That's the one who's buying," he said.

"Bourbon," his friend told the bartender.

I loved it. Those people in Culbertson had a live one and they knew it. All the drinks for the next few hours couldn't have cost me more than maybe twenty-five dollars, which I considered a bargain. When the train whistle blew, I knew I'd be leaving in a few minutes.

"I've got to go," I said, leaving some money on the bar, "but set up the house one more time."

Something like that never happens when you travel by plane. And if you're late and miss a plane, you're stranded until the next flight. With a train, sometimes you can be late and still catch it. One time I was in New York at a CBS taping and was supposed to leave for Chicago on the Lake Shore Limited out of Grand Central. Thinking that the taping might take longer than planned, I had a car and driver ready. When the taping session ended, I knew we would never get through the crosstown traffic to Grand Central in time, so we started driving north along the Hudson River on roads as close as we could get to the railroad tracks. We thought we might be able to catch the train at Harmon, but we just missed it. We missed it at Poughkeepsie too. But at Albany the Lake Shore Limited was sitting in the old station there, waiting for me. It always sits in Albany for about half an hour to put on cars from a train out of Boston.

"What a way to travel," I told the conductor. "When a plane leaves New York for Chicago, you can't catch it at Albany!"

I know quite a few conductors by now. One of my favorites was Elwood Best, who would get on the California Zephyr in Denver and stay on to McCook, Nebraska, where he lived. Every so often he would phone ahead to Tony and Patty's Speakeasy in McCook that I was on the train. When we stopped there, Elwood and I would hurry across the street to the Speakeasy where cans of Miller Lite (yes, I really do drink the stuff) would be on ice in a champagne bucket along with a hot-sausage sandwich. One time a photographer from the *McCook Gazette* was there to record our arrival.

Another great conductor was Emery Miller, who was really a play-by-play railroad announcer.

"In another few minutes," Emery would say, "we will be stopping in Laramie, Wyoming, the Gem City of the West."

On the way in and out of Laramie, he would tell us all about its history, its characters, and its famous people.

"Over to the left," he would say, "is the hill where Steamboat was born, the meanest rodeo horse there ever was. He was ridden only one time and that was by Old Jake, who's deceased now—but back in 1905 he rode Steamboat, only man to ever do that. On the left up here you'll see a tepee. An old Indian squaw lives there. She washes her clothes in the Laramie River, which runs nearby. She also has a red jeep that she uses to go into town to do her grocery shopping."

And he would point out the squaw, with her red jeep parked outside the tepee.

"Laramie, the Gem City of the West," he would continue, "is also the home of pro football's meanest player, Conrad Dobler. You have to be mean to live in Laramie, the Gem City of the West. I guess that's why he's the meanest player in pro football. And sportscaster Curt Gowdy, who's one of the finest fly-fishermen in the country, grew up in Laramie, the Gem City of the West."

More conductors should do that. It would make the trip a lot more interesting, especially for first-time travelers.

And more bartenders should be like Bob, who used to be on the Zephyr when I first started traveling by train. Bob could keep a party going all night in the club car with his chatter.

After I'm talked out in the club car, I like to go back to the privacy of my bedroom. Even for a big guy like me, a deluxe bedroom on the trains west of Chicago is as spacious as you could expect, about seven feet by seven feet with a wide, upholstered seat that turns into a lower berth and an upper berth. The room also has an upholstered chair next to the window, a small metal sink, and a combination toilet-shower stall with two buttons. Press the lower button, the toilet flushes. Press the button just above it, water sprays down out of the shower nozzle. (Every so often I've been soaked when I pressed the top button by mistake.) On the trains east of Chicago, a bedroom is slightly smaller.

In my berth, I like to read my newspapers and magazines, especially during the NFL season. That's when I do my homework on the teams playing in my next TV game. I study their media guides, their news releases, the latest newspaper stories about them. I don't take notes. I've always had good recall.

I always sleep well on a train, sometimes ten or twelve hours. I once heard a passenger—who sounded like a doctor—explaining why the rolling movement of a train actually helps you sleep. Being on a train, I remember him saying, is similar to a baby being in the womb. Maybe that's why I sleep better on a train than I do in a hotel.

In the morning, I usually sleep until the last call for breakfast before going into the dining car—staggering into it actually. On a fast-moving train everybody staggers instead of walks. The trick is to keep your feet wide apart, your toes pointed straight ahead, your shoulders squared, your knees flexed. That way you can roll with the roll.

I always prefer the last call for lunch and dinner, too. By then nobody is waiting for the table I'm at, so I can take my time. I'm told that years ago dining-car food was as good as in many fine restaurants. It's not that good anymore. It's the same menu on every train, but it's still better than airline food. For breakfast, I usually order pancakes. For lunch, a cheeseburger and chili. For dinner, a steak or roast beef—unless we're going through Colorado, where stuffed trout always seems to be on the menu as an extra.

My first few years on trains, the crew occasionally invited me to eat dinner with them if they had something special—red beans and rice, ox tails and hot dogs, sweet-potato pie, things like that. The cooks had big stoves then. Now they mostly use microwave ovens.

One thing I've learned—always wear a dark shirt on a train. When you're eating on a moving train, you tend to spill things.

Even though I'm a little cooped up in a train, it's not like in a plane. If the train is stopping in Denver for, say, twenty minutes, I know I've got time to call Virginia and the boys and buy a newspaper.

Now that I've had time to think about it, I've realized that I've had a few claustrophobic tendencies ever since I was a kid. At dinner, I had to sit at one end of the table or the other, not in the middle. At a movie, I always sat on the aisle. In an elevator, I was always uneasy. But other than that, no kid ever had a better time growing up than I did.

I was born in Austin, Minnesota, on April 10, 1936, but we moved to Daly City, just across from the San Francisco line, not far from the Pacific Ocean, when I was six—my father Earl, my mother Mary, and my two younger sisters, Dolores and Judy. My mother was very religious. For years I thought you had to go to Tuesday evening devotions just like you did Sunday mass. My dad was an auto mechanic at Les Vogel's Chevrolet, but he hated his job. That's probably why he never pushed me to get a job when I was a teenager.

"Don't start working until you have to," he told me. "Once you do, that's it."

Our house was at 213 Knowles Street, with a little empty lot behind it. Madden's lot, the other kids called it. I played my first football and baseball there. Then I discovered Marchbank Park down in a pretty tree-shaded hollow. It had a grass field with a real dirt baseball diamond. On the low walls beneath the slopes around it, signs read "Keep Off Bank." (Those signs are still there.) I spent more time in that park than I did at home. I was a batboy there for the Sarto A.C., which meant I got all the old baseballs and splintered bats. Hammer a nail into the bat, tape it up and you can use it again.

My first baseball team was the Daly City Red Sox. At Jefferson High School I played football, baseball, and basketball. At night, I hung out on the streetcorner or at the pool hall with John Robinson, Ray Rosa, George Schreiber, Al Figone, and George McLeod.

John Robinson and I were always big on being somebody when we were playing ball, meaning somebody else—one of the 49ers or one of the Seals, which was San Francisco's baseball team in the Pacific Coast League then. I was always Bob Toneff, the 49ers' big offensive tackle, which meant I wore number 74. That's how we started thinking about how certain people had to wear certain numbers. Certain numbers just fit them—77 for Red Grange and 98 for Tommy Harmon, and later on 32 for Jim Brown and O.J. Simpson in football, 44 for Hank Aaron in baseball.

Billy Martin is a 1. To wear 1, you have to be small and tough but you have to be good. You can't be little and bad. You have to be little, but you have to play big.

Dom DiMaggio was always the perfect 2 to me. To wear 2, a player has to be good, but he's more mind and gamesmanship than fighter. Dom DiMaggio always had that little owl look that a 2 needs. Bob Griese wore 12 with the Miami Dolphins, but if he had been a baseball player, he would have been a 2—glasses, cerebral.

To wear 3, you should be a big guy, like Babe Ruth was, like Daryle Lamonica was as the Raiders' quarterback, like Dale Murphy of the Atlanta Braves.

To wear 9, a guy has to be good, tall and with a little hunchback in him. Ted Williams was a great 9, he hunched a little in his batting stance. But there's a number for everybody. Sometimes when I think about famous people, I try to decide what their number would be if they were football players. To me, Pope John Paul II would be a 73, Ronald Reagan a 16, Henry Kissinger a 22, Johnny Carson a 12.

Around that time when John Robinson and I were thinking about numbers, my dad bought me an old black 1940 Cadillac to drive around. It looked like a hearse. But if I got in a wreck—which I never did—he didn't want me in a little flimsy car.

I never had a job as such, but I always had a little money in my pocket from caddying. At first, I made $1.50 a bag for an eighteen-hole loop at Lake Merced Country Club on Sunday mornings. Then Lefty O'Doul, the great hitter who was a member there, would take a bunch of us to the Seals' baseball game that afternoon in his Cadillac convertible. I later caddied at the San Francisco Golf Club, where every so often I shagged balls for Ken Venturi, who would win the 1964 U.S. Open championship. I got five dollars for a loop there.

Walking along with the members under those beautiful oak and eucalyptus trees, I realized that the reason they all had money was because they were college graduates, Stanford and Cal mostly. That's when I put it in my head never to quit school.

Not that I had ever been a scholar—an altar boy, yes, but not a scholar. At our grammar school reunion

43

at Our Lady of Perpetual Help a few years ago, I was still afraid of Sister Jacqueline, the sixth-grade teacher who always whopped me across the hands with her wooden pointer. All those nuns taught me discipline— things you could do, things you couldn't do. The most scared I've ever been was the day Sister Superior—I never knew her name, just Sister Superior—wanted to talk to my parents about me one night. When my dad got home from work, he never liked to go out, much less get dressed up to go out to see Sister Superior about me. When he and my mom got home, he was even more annoyed.

"John," he said, "that nun told us you talk in class too much."

I'm sure I did talk too much. And now CBS pays me to talk thanks to my being able to get to the games by train. Aside from those few little claustrophobic tendencies I had as a kid, I think the Cal Poly plane crash in 1960 probably had a subconscious effect on my attitude toward planes.

During the 1960 season, two years after I played at Cal Poly, their football team boarded a chartered twin-engine C-46 at the Toledo, Ohio, airport after a 50–6 loss to Bowling Green. Moments after takeoff in a dense fog, the plane exploded. Of the forty-four people on board, twenty-two died, including sixteen players, a student manager, and a booster-club member.

I thought about that crash for a long time. Quite a few of those who were killed were good friends of mine.

Even so, I flew when I had to. But not when I didn't have to, not if I had a choice. One time when I was an assistant coach at San Diego State an assistant athletic director fouled up the travel plans for our first road game, which had Don Coryell, the head coach, steaming. I happened to be in Don's office when the assistant athletic director tried to explain, but Don didn't want an explanation.

"Don't handle our trips anymore," Don snapped. "Don't do it, understand?..."

Don was groping now. He realized that he needed somebody to arrange the travel.

"Just don't do it anymore," Don said. Then he turned to me. "John will handle it now."

My first assignment was to arrange the travel plans for our game at Northern Arizona in Flagstaff up in the mountains not far from the Grand Canyon—beautiful country but remote. An airline rep suggested that we fly to Phoenix in a big jet, then transfer to two small prop planes for the trip up to Flagstaff, whose airport had a short runway.

"I don't think Don would like that," I said.

I didn't know if Don would like it or not, but I knew I didn't like the idea of putting the team on two small planes—especially since I would be on one of those two small planes. The next day, I checked the railroad timetables. To get to Flagstaff, we could take a chartered bus to San Bernardino, then board a train for the overnight ride to Flagstaff.

"Every kid should travel overnight on a train," I told Don. "It'll be an educational experience for them."

I don't know if Don was listening. He probably was thinking about a new play. But he nodded, so we went to Flagstaff and back on the train. I don't think I slept on a train again until 1979, after I was the first coach chosen to receive the Vince Lombardi Dedication Award at a Milwaukee dinner. I was tired of being uncomfortable on planes. I phoned Amtrak for a reservation on the California Zephyr out of Oakland for Chicago, a fifty-one-hour trip that I've taken dozens of times since. I get on the train at Martinez, a little fishing village half an hour out of Oakland, at about one in the afternoon. Two days later, it pulls into Union Station in Chicago around four in the afternoon—if it's on time, which it seldom is.

The day before I left, Bob King, who had been sports information director at San Diego State before moving to the Denver Nuggets of the NBA, phoned to say hello.

"You won't believe this," I said, "but I'm going to be in Denver the day after tomorrow. The train stops there. Come down to the station and I'll buy you a beer."

Sure enough, when I got off the train and walked into the Denver station, Bob and Steve Cameron, then a sports columnist for the *Denver Post,* were waiting for me. But we couldn't find a bar in the station.

"Let's go back to the train," I said. "We'll have a beer in the club car."

Jesse the bartender opened three cans and we sat there, drinking beer and talking. On the second beer, I suggested that they stay on the train to Chicago with me. And they agreed. Neither one had a toothbrush, much less a ticket. But that night and the next day we had a great time. When we got to Chicago, they hurried to catch a flight back to Denver—but not before they set up a deal with me. Since they had stayed overnight on the train with me, I had to stop in Denver on my way back and stay overnight with them. The night I arrived there, we went to a Nuggets game, then to the bar atop the Holiday Inn where I was staying. By now Bob had organized a party of about a dozen guys—Nuggets people, some sportswriters, some friends. As each one joined us, Bob explained how I had stopped in Denver after being in Milwaukee to receive the Vince Lombardi Award.

"Go get your trophy," Bob kept suggesting. "Everybody wants to see your trophy."

I kept saying no, but he finally talked me into giving him the key to my room. And my trophy was passed around for inspection by everybody at our table. Which was all right, a little embarrassing, but all right. Bob then used the trophy to make a drink known as a Moose River Hummer—equal parts Galliano, peppermint schnapps, and 151-proof rum.

"Ask the waitress," I heard somebody say, "to bring a bottle of each."

Pretty soon all that booze was splashing into my Vince Lombardi award, my beautiful silver bowl. It's too late for me to say anything. I'm just hoping it doesn't develop into too bad a scene. Just then Bob tossed a match into the bowl and, whoom, the flames jumped five, six feet.

After a few seconds, the flames disappeared, but smoke was curling up from my bowl—which now was more blackish than beautiful.

I just sat there and took a deep breath and looked around. I thought about what a waste of time it had been to go all the way to Milwaukee to get a trophy I'd never be able to show anybody. Virginia won't believe this. Vince Lombardi must be turning over in his grave. All those nice people in Milwaukee, if they could see the trophy now.

When the smoke cleared, the guys started passing the bowl around the way hockey players do when they win the Stanley Cup—to take a drink from it.

Around and around it went for about an hour, one or two swallows at a time. I'm not a big drinker, but I even took a couple of gulps. About the third time around, one guy took a big gulp, put the bowl down, leaned back in his chair and toppled backwards onto the floor.

"That's just Ralph," somebody said. "He'll be all right in the morning."

When my trophy was empty, the guys started to drift out. The party was over. I took my blackened silver trophy back to my room. The next day I got on the train to Oakland to go home. As soon as I got into the house, Virginia opened up the trophy box. I heard her gasp.

"What is this," she said, "a barbecue?"

She spent the whole day cleaning it up, but it's never been as shiny as it was when I received it. Never will be.

4

Not the Lawyer Type

DURING MY TWO YEARS AS A RAIDER ASSISTANT coach, the team went to Super Bowl II and then to the AFL championship game. But after I took over as head coach in 1969, we lost our first three exhibition games. Some of the Oakland fans were beginning to wonder if Al Davis had picked the wrong coach. Around that time Virginia was at a party where one of the women realized I was her husband.

"Oh," she said to Virginia, "you're married to the man we're all going to lynch."

I never got lynched. I never had a losing season in my ten years there. But a coach has to live with constant scrutiny. That was all right with me. I was a coach because I wanted to be. I had to take the bad with the good. For me, there was always more good than bad, always more fun than frustration. But then I was luckier than most coaches. I had great players and a great organization. I also had started coaching early. I was only twenty-three when I went back to Cal Poly in San Luis Obispo with a bad knee that had ended my chances of making the Philadelphia Eagles in 1959 as a rookie guard.

In one of my first scrimmages as a pro at training camp, a ball-carrier fell across my left leg, tearing ligaments and cartilage in the knee.

"It's a bad one," the Eagles' doctor told me. "You need an operation. You won't play this year, but maybe you can next year."

Maybe next year. That didn't sound too good. My knee operation started me thinking seriously about coaching, especially when I sat with Norm Van Brocklin as he studied opponents' game films. At the time "Dutch" was one of the NFL's best quarterbacks, a future Hall of Famer who would lead the Eagles to the 1960 championship. The day I had arrived in Hershey, Pennsylvania, where the Eagles trained, I was on line for equipment when I realized Dutch was in front of me. I thought, *hey, I really am in the NFL now.*

But when I had surgery, suddenly I was no longer in the NFL, except that the Eagles kept me in Philadelphia all season taking treatment for my knee. Every morning before practice, I would get to Franklin Field about 8:30 so I'd be out of the whirlpool before the real players needed it. Dutch was the only other player there that early. He sat in a dark little room watching films of our next opponent. After my treatment one morning I wandered into that little room and stood in the back watching the black-and-white films flicker on the screen. Dutch looked around.

"Hey, Red," he said, "c'mon in and sit down."

After that, I sat with Dutch Van Brocklin almost

every morning. Not that we were buddies. My room-mate Darrell Aschbacher, a rookie guard from Oregon, had an older brother who knew Dutch, so I had gotten to know him a little. As he watched the films, Dutch would tell me what he was thinking, what he was looking for in our next opponent's defense.

"The idea," he said, "is to let your backs and receivers do what they do best in taking advantage of the other defense."

That year the Eagles had Clarence Peaks at half-back and Billy Barnes at fullback. Tommy McDonald, Bobby Walston were the wide receivers, Pete Retzlaff the tight end. Watching the films, Dutch would run them over and over again to see where he could use Peaks on outside runs and use Barnes inside. He liked to use McDonald deep, Walston short, and Retzlaff over the middle.

"Every defense is a little different," he would say. "You've got to attack it a little different."

I just watched and listened. Until then, I didn't know much about football except for what I did as a lineman on offense and defense. But sitting in that little room, I learned how to attack and how to defend. I learned the basic philosophy of being a coach. It's a good thing I did. I never played another game. I had an offer to join the Los Angeles Chargers in 1960, the AFL's first season. But they didn't realize I couldn't run. I had a brace on my knee. About all I could do was return to Cal Poly for my master's degree.

"And for a fate worse than death," Virginia likes to say, "marriage."

I always tell people I met Virginia at Cal Poly, but she tells the truth. "We met in a bar," she says. "Harry's, in Pismo Beach, a nice bar." We got engaged before I went to the Eagles' training camp. Now I was hoping to get into graduate school at Cal Poly for a master's degree in education, with an emphasis on physical education. But the chairman of the phys-ed department, Bob Mott, not only didn't like me, he tried to talk Virginia out of marrying me.

"When John was here before," he told her, "he never worked on his studies."

Professor Mott was right. I had been too busy playing football and too busy hanging out in Bobby Beathard's room—the same Bobby Beathard who is now the Redskins' general manager, who put together their Super Bowl XVII champions. He was our quarterback. In our dorm, I roomed with Pat Lovell, a lineman who is now an Olympic wrestling official—but our room was always a mess of dirty clothes. Across the hall, Bobby's room was always spotless, so I hung out there.

"You can't study all the time," I'd tell Bobby, "you've got to relax once in a while."

We both relaxed, but not just once in a while. More like most of the time. I wasn't much of a student then. After high school, I had thought about being a lawyer so I just started going to colleges. I played football at San Mateo Junior College, then I transferred to the University of Oregon, then I heard about Grays Harbor College in Aberdeen, Washington, so I went there for a semester. The football coach, Chace Anderson, arranged jobs for his players. Mine was to sweep out the Mint Cafe in town. The more I traveled, the more I realized later that almost every small town in America has a Mint Cafe.

But the Mint Cafe in Aberdeen had a card room in the back—a few green felt-topped tables where the lumberjacks and fish-cannery workers played draw poker, low ball, and fan tan.

My first few days there, the boss liked the way I mixed with the poker players. After that, I was more of a shill than a sweeper. But that's where I really learned to play poker, which I still play at a moment's notice. But the more I bounced around colleges, I realized I wasn't the lawyer type. All my life all I had done was play football and baseball. I was a pretty good catcher. My senior year at Jefferson Union High School in Daly City, the Yankees and the Red Sox wanted to sign me to play in the minors for seventy-five dollars a month. I played baseball at Cal Poly until the Eagles drafted me. I thought I was going to play football forever. That's the trouble with most good athletes. They never think it's going to end. But for me, it suddenly had ended even before it started. As much as I didn't like Bob Mott telling Virginia to break our engagement, I respected him. He was a tough, no-nonsense professor. Even though the education department had accepted my application, he had to approve it on behalf of the phys-ed department. That meant an interview.

"I know I didn't study as much as I should've," I told him. "I didn't think I'd be back here so soon. I thought I'd be playing pro football for a few years. But now that I am back, I'll work hard for my master's."

I guess he realized I meant it. I not only earned my master's, I wound up only a few credits short of a doctorate. As a coach, the class that helped me the most was child psychology. I learned that, as a group, football players react like children. If you take any player out of the group, he wouldn't be bothered by the things that bother the group. For instance, when I was coaching, before a road trip I always read through our itinerary. I wanted the players to hear how long the flight took, how long the bus ride to the hotel took. I didn't want them to be confused or surprised. If our flight to San Diego took an hour the week before, some players would get restless after an hour unless they had been alerted that the flight to Miami this week would take six hours. Some of our bus rides to the hotel were only twenty minutes, but in Boston it was forty-five minutes. If they thought it should have taken only thirty minutes, some players would start bitching.

"How come we're not there, coach?" somebody would yell. "What's goin' on here, coach, we can't play here."

But if they were told about our travel schedule in advance, they usually were fine. In addition to taking classes at Cal Poly that spring semester, I did my practice teaching at San Luis Obispo High School, where Phil Prijatel was the athletic director. Soon after I went there, it was time for spring football practice. But there were no coaches. The staff had been let go after the previous season and the new coach, Jack Frost, had to stay at his high school until the semester ended.

"You want to be a coach someday," Phil said to me. "Suppose you run spring football."

For three weeks, I coached the whole team by myself. No assistants. No money and no teaching credits either, but I loved it. Every afternoon Phil would come over and watch practice, but I did all the coaching. Phil had a son, Phil, Jr., a running back who was being recruited that year by Al Baldock, the coach at Allan Hancock Junior College in Santa Maria, California.

"I'm looking for a line coach," Al told Phil one night. "You know anybody?"

"I've got just the guy for you," Phil said. "He's running our spring practice."

Al hired me. I was really a coach now. My first year there as an assistant, we were 10–0, winning the Orange Show Bowl. My second year we were 8–1 before losing the Prune Bowl. But then Al left. The athletic director, Joe White, named me head coach. My first year we were 4–5, but in my second we improved to 8–1.

In those years, I decided that my personality was more like Vince Lombardi's than that of Weeb Ewbank, Sid Gillman, or Blanton Collier, the other old masters of that era.

I also admired the way Lombardi had built the Packers into the NFL's dominant team, thinking that if I ever got a chance to be a pro coach, I'd want to build a team too. One year, a coaches' clinic at the University of Nevada in Reno advertised that Lombardi would be lecturing there. I signed up. I'll always remember the title of his lecture: The Green Bay Sweep. That's all, just The Green Bay Sweep, the play that Paul Hornung ran with Jim Taylor and the two guards, Jerry Kramer and Fuzzy Thurston, blocking for him. As we filed into the lecture hall that day, I didn't expect to be there long. After all, how long could even Vince Lombardi talk about one play.

Eight hours, that's how long! Four hours in the morning, break for lunch. Four more hours in the afternoon.

He stood up there at the blackboard with a piece of chalk and dissected the Green Bay sweep player-by-player—each player's assignment against every possible defense, against every possible stunt, against every possible blitz, against every possible coverage. As he talked, I kept diagramming the variations of the play and taking notes.

Sitting in the front row of the 150 coaches, Sid Gillman was doing the same thing—as well as asking questions.

Going into the lecture, I thought I knew everything there was to know about football. But suddenly I realized I didn't have any depth to my knowledge. In those years, I might have been able to talk for half an hour on one play. But not eight hours. Nowhere near eight hours. After that I went to all the clinics I could. At one, I learned about the "I-formation" that John McKay popularized with O.J. Simpson at tailback for Southern Cal long before he was the Tampa Bay Bucs' coach. But during his lecture, John acknowledged that he had not designed the "I-formation."

"The coach who put it in our play book is sitting right here," John said. "Stand up, Don."

Don Coryell had been the SC backfield coach in 1960, but by now he was San Diego State's head coach. After the lecture, John McKay was surrounded by young college and high-school coaches wanting to ask him more questions, but I thought, *If McKay learned the "I-formation" from Coryell, then I'd rather talk to Coryell about it.* I was the only guy who went over to where Don was sitting. That's how I got to know him. When he was recruiting in Santa Maria later on, he stayed with Virginia and me at our house. We talked football, diagrammed plays. When his defensive coordinator, Tom Bass, left San Diego State to join the Chargers in 1964, Don offered me that job. By then I was ready for that level of coaching—not just the football part but also the teaching part.

Coaching is teaching. Some coaches try to make

what they do sound mysterious and complicated when it's not. It's just football. But to be a good coach, you have to be a good teacher.

After getting my master's degree, I taught health, recreation and phys-ed at Hancock Junior College and San Diego State for six years. Not as intellectual as philosophy or Shakespearean literature, but it helped prepare me to be a coach. I learned how to get up in front of a group, present something, and get it done. In preparing for class, a teacher has to be organized. Once in the classroom, a teacher has to get the students to settle down, to pay attention, to understand. After you teach, you discuss and then you test. Coaching football is basically the same thing. You teach in meetings. You discuss on the practice field. You test in the game.

At San Diego State, I learned there was something else to coaching football in college—recruiting. We had great weather there, a terrific football program. My three years there with Don Coryell, the Aztecs were 8–2, 8–2, and then 11–0 as the nation's number one small-college team. Even though the Aztecs were in what was known then as the NCAA's college division, we could recruit against just about any school except Southern Cal, especially when Mike Garrett won the 1965 Heisman Trophy there. I'd really work to get a player from a junior college or high school. I'd talk to his parents, talk to his girlfriend, talk to his coach, talk to his principal. But if SC wanted him, he went there and never looked back. Sometimes never even thanked me. I eventually made a deal with Craig Fertig, a former SC quarterback, who then was an assistant coach supervising their recruiting of junior-college players.

"Do me a favor," I said. "Just tell me the eight or ten guys you're interested in."

Craig agreed. After that, we checked with him before putting together our list of maybe two dozen junior-college players. But one year we had Haven Moses, a wide receiver who later played with the Buffalo Bills and the Denver Broncos, on our list. Haven was at Harbor Junior College in Los Angeles, right in SC's lap. When I phoned Craig for his list, sure enough, Haven was on it. But this time I didn't back off. As a wide receiver, Haven liked Don Coryell's passing offense. One night Craig phoned, all in a huff.

"I hear you're still after Haven," he said. "I thought you were supposed to lay off those kids I told you we wanted."

"No, no, that wasn't the deal," I said. "The deal was that you would tell me who was on your list. I didn't say that we wouldn't still *try* to get a player who was on your list."

"Well, we really want him."

"We really want him, too."

We got him. We also got Fred Dryer, later a Pro Bowl defensive end for the Los Angeles Rams. At the time, the city of San Diego was building what is now known as Jack Murphy Stadium where the Chargers, Aztecs, and the baseball Padres play. One day I drove Fred over to Mission Valley where they had begun the excavation. I parked the car nearby and we walked down into this huge hole in the ground.

"You'll be playing right here," I told him, waving my arms, "and that hole over there, that's where you'll be coming out of the tunnel from the locker room with sixty thousand people cheering you."

Fred told me later that I had pictured the locker room at the wrong end from where it was built.

When the Aztecs went 11–0 in 1966, I had started thinking about becoming a head coach by the time I was thirty-five—but I was just thinking college then, not the pros. That season, Don Coryell was considering the Arizona job. If he went there, I heard that I would get the head job at SD State. But Don stayed. Even so, I thought I should go through the experience of applying for a head job. I knew the Utah State job was open, so I phoned the athletic director there out of the blue. As it turned out, I was one of the last three people to be considered, which surprised me. The jobs at Cal Poly (Pomona) and Cal Western also were open, but I didn't want to be a head coach just to be a head coach. I wanted the right spot. I was happy at San Diego State, especially with Don still there. So when Virginia told me one night that John Rauch of the Oakland Raiders had phoned, I didn't think much about it.

"I'll call him tomorrow morning," I said.

"No, he wants you to call tonight," she said. "He specifically mentioned tonight."

"He just wants some information, like Tom Fears did."

Around that time Tom was putting together the New Orleans Saints' first coaching staff for the 1967 season. When he phoned, I thought sure he was going to offer me a job, but he just wanted me to rate some free agents for him. I figured John Rauch wanted the same type of information.

"No, no," Virginia insisted, "this sounded important."

I phoned John, who told me that the Raiders were expanding their coaching staff. They wanted somebody to work with the linebackers. I went up to Oakland, where John interviewed me. The next thing I knew, I had the job. The following year I was contacted about the head job at Cal Poly in San Luis Obispo, but I wasn't interested. The year before I would have taken it. Going back to my alma mater, that would have been perfect. But even after the Raiders lost Super Bowl II to the Green Bay Packers, 33–14, my first season, I knew I wanted to be a head coach in the NFL, not in college. In college a head coach has to be involved with recruiting, with alumni, with booster clubs. But in the NFL a head coach just has to coach. That's all I wanted to do—coach.

My first year on the Raider staff, I wanted to coach so much at rookie camp I wore down a linebacker, Duane Benson, out of Hamline College in St. Paul, Minnesota.

As the linebacker coach, I had prepared a long list of drills for all my linebackers. But in rookie camp, Duane was my only linebacker. I didn't care. I had him doing all the drills over and over—hitting the tackling dummies, jumping over the tackling dummies, hitting the sled, standing broad jumps, doing the ball drill, the mirror drill, the reaction drill. As soon as he finished one drill, I started him on another. I never gave the kid a breather. He had come to camp at about 225, but by the time the veterans arrived, he was down to 210 and gasping. He made the club anyway.

I was really excited about everything that year, especially when we went to New York to play the Jets with Joe Namath at Shea Stadium on a Saturday night before sixty-three thousand people.

On our chartered bus taking us from JFK to our

midtown hotel, I was sitting with Kent McCloughan, one of our cornerbacks. I had never been in New York City before, so I was gaping at the Empire State Building and all the other skyscrapers.

"This is great," I said, nudging Kent.

"I don't think it's so great," he said, staring at the floor of the bus. "I hate to play here."

"Whaddya mean, this is great, this is pro football."

"The hell it is," he said. "I hate it here. I just hate it. If I didn't play football, I'd never come here. I hate Shea Stadium. I hate Maynard."

"Oh, that," I said.

I knew now what he meant. As an All-AFL cornerback, Kent usually put Lance Alworth of the Chargers in his pocket but Don Maynard of the Jets drove him crazy. At a game in Oakland the next year Maynard caught 10 passes for 228 yards, still a Jets' record. So there I was, riding into New York for the first time and sitting next to a cornerback who hated thinking about having to cover a wide receiver who had his number. Kent had completely deflated me but I got excited again when Al Davis took the coaching staff to dinner at Toots Shor's restaurant. After we sat down, Toots himself appeared at our table. Al introduced everybody.

"Madden, that's a good name," he said in that gravel voice. "Owney Madden was a pal of mine."

Owney Madden, I discovered, was a famous bootlegger during Prohibition when Toots was a bouncer in a New York speakeasy. Toots apparently thought we were related. He started telling Owney Madden stories. The next night, the game wasn't as much fun as Toots's stories. The Jets beat us, 27 – 14, but by the time we went to New York again in 1969, I was the head coach. Make that: I was *learning* how to be the head coach—learning as I went along, learning from other people's advice, learning from what I remembered.

The day I was announced as the Raider coach, I got several congratulatory phone calls. One was from Red Hickey, who had installed the "shotgun" offense with the 49ers a decade earlier. I had gotten to know Red when I was at San Diego State.

"I just want to tell you one thing," Red said on the phone that day. "You're the head coach, it's your football team. Coach the team yourself, don't give it away. Not even a part of it. Don't give the offense to an assistant, or the defense or the special teams or the quarterbacks. Keep it all yourself. If you keep it, you can always give away a little of it any time you want, but if you give a big piece of it away, you can never get it back."

When the Raiders opened with a loss, a tie, and a loss my second year as head coach, I remembered Vince Lombardi's philosophy when your team is struggling.

"To be a good coach," Vince once said, "you have to be the opposite of what you feel. When your team is going bad, you want to get on their ass but that's when everybody else is on their ass. Their family, their friends, the fans, the media, the guy in the grocery store. That's when you need to pat 'em on the back, to tell 'em to just keep working hard and everything will be all right. Conversely, when everything is going good, you don't have to pat 'em on the back because everybody else is. That's when you have to be tough."

After those two losses and a tie, I didn't hold a meeting and chew out my players. I cringe when I read about coaches calling a big meeting to chew out a team in a slump. I just patted my players on the back, like Vince had suggested. The rest of the season we lost only two games. I had good players. That always helps. But so did Vince Lombardi's philosophy.

I learned from my mistakes, from decisions that went wrong. But looking back, I think I learned more from people. Even as far back as when I was the Hancock coach. My first year as head coach there, I thought all my players should be really serious before a game, probably because as a player I had always been really serious before a game. I couldn't accept it when some of my players turned on music and told jokes as they sat at their lockers before a game. Especially my fullback, Blair Sheldon.

"Hey, this is serious," I yelled. "Football is serious."

They turned the music off and stopped telling jokes. They got real serious, just the way I wanted them to be. When we won the game, I thought I had done the right thing. But before the next game, Blair Sheldon stopped in my office. (Years later, Larry Csonka reminded me of Blair, who wasn't as big as "Zonk" but just as tough.)

"Coach," he said, "there are all different kinds of personalities in that locker room before a game. Everybody wants to win the same way but there are different ways of preparing to win. Some guys take a nap, some go to the bathroom, some throw up, some listen to music. Some, like me, tell jokes. We're not all the same."

"Let me think about that," I said.

The more I thought about it, the more I realized Blair was right. After that, I always had two locker rooms at Hancock—one for the quiet guys, one for the guys who liked to play music or tell jokes. On the

Raiders, we had several guys who always got to the stadium early on game day to play cards—Fred Biletnikoff, Willie Brown, Jack Tatum, George Atkinson, Dave Dalby, Skip Thomas, Otis Sistrunk.

I've always felt that the fewer rules a coach has, the fewer rules there are for the players to break. My two years as an assistant coach, many coaches in pro football had a rule that players had to wear a coat and tie when the team traveled. But I threw out that rule. Their idea was that their teams would look nice to strangers who saw them. But hardly anybody sees a team travel. On a typical road trip, our players would gather at the Oakland Airport, get on a chartered jet to, say, Denver, then get on a chartered bus from the airport there to the hotel, then go to their rooms. Maybe a few people would see them at the airport and in the hotel lobby. Big deal. Maybe it was because I didn't particularly like a coat and tie, but I preferred my players to be comfortable when they traveled. I never agreed with coaches who thought that a coat and tie develop discipline, or with coaches who thought that rules against long hair, beards, or sideburns developed discipline.

To me, discipline in football occurs on the field, not off it. Discipline is knowing what you're supposed to do and doing it as best you can. On the field, the Raiders were, and are, a disciplined team. On third down and short yardage, the Raiders don't jump off-side. That's discipline—not a coat and tie, not a clean shave. I had only three rules on the Raiders—be on time, pay attention, and play like hell when I tell you to.

The older a coach gets, the more he needs someone as a go-between with the players to make sure the coach knows how the players like to wear their clothes and their hair in order to be fashionable. Especially the younger players. I was thirty-two when I took over the Raiders, as young or almost as young as most of my players. By the time I stopped coaching, I was almost a generation older than most of them.

Looking back now, I was lucky I stopped when I did. I got out before the NFL's drug problem developed.

Maybe I was naive or maybe there was a generation gap, but if any of my players were sniffing cocaine, I never suspected it. For one thing, back in 1978, my last season as coach, not many players were making enough money to afford cocaine. Back then, $100,000 was a big salary, $50,000 was the average. Most of my players had wives and kids and mortgages. They didn't have the money or the time for cocaine. Around the time I became head coach, amphetamines were big with some teams. But then the NFL demanded copies of all bills for medical supplies. Then the players got the word that if they needed emergency surgery for, say, a knee after having taken amphetamines before that game, they could die on the operating table. I don't think many took pills after that.

I've always felt that if a player works hard to get in shape and stays in shape, he doesn't need any pills.

Back when I was coaching, I never heard of any drug dealers being around my players. But one time Al Davis's executive assistant, Al LoCasale, informed me that a known gambler named Nick Dudich had been "seen with" Kenny Stabler, whatever that meant. Kenny was always nice to anyone and everyone. He always made it easy for somebody to hang out with him. Maybe too easy. As soon as Al LoCasale told me about it, I told the team.

"We don't want this guy around anymore," I said. "If anyone has been inviting him around, don't invite him anymore. If he's seen around here, he's going to be run off."

That too is discipline. Too many coaches want to be "one of the guys" but that's the worst thing a coach can be. Your players don't need another friend. Your players have all the friends they need. Sometimes too many. Your players need someone to tell them what to do. Your players need a coach, a teacher—not a friend.

That doesn't mean a coach shouldn't be friendly with his players. By being friendly, I mean talking to as many players as possible each day if possible—except game day. I stayed away from my players on game day. I was a basket case. I didn't want to add to a player's natural nervousness. But the other days I tried to talk to each of them, usually in the locker room or the trainer's room. Sometimes it was merely a quick, "How ya doin'." Sometimes it was a conversation. But by talking to every player every day, if they wanted to tell me something, it wasn't difficult for them to approach me. And by talking to them every day, they didn't feel something was up when I would stop to talk to them. Every so often, of course, I had to chew out a player. About a week after one of those scenes, one of my favorite players, offensive tackle Henry Lawrence, spoke up.

"How come you're still mad at me?" he said.

"I'm not mad at you," I said. "What makes you think I'm mad at you?"

"You haven't been talking to me."

"I've said hello to you every day."

"But all you say is hello," he said. "You're not talking to me. You're still mad from the other day."

"Henry, I forgot about that as soon as it was over."

I really had. I never carried a grudge against a player, at least not in my mind. After we talked it out, it was over. I had words at one time or another with probably every player I've ever had. But that's what I meant about the players needing somebody to tell them what to do. Sometimes I had to tell them again and again. In coaching, as in teaching, repetition is so important, especially for offensive plays. You have to tell the players what you want, you have to put it on a blackboard, you have to walk through it, you have to go through it at half-speed, then you have to run through it at full speed. After all that, you have to keep doing it over and over until everybody's got it right.

"You can only go as fast," I remember Vince Lombardi saying at a clinic, "as your slowest learner."

Even so, I never tried to keep football simple. If your offense is simple, it's simple to stop. If your defense is simple, it's simple to attack. Simple things are for simple people. Not that my players were nuclear scientists, but they were football-smart. That's why we usually had good practices. Just because the players are grunting or talking it up doesn't mean it's a good practice. No mistakes—that's a good practice. And just because the players are growling in the locker room before a game doesn't mean they'll have a good game. They might stink out the joint. When they're laughing before a game, it doesn't mean they're too relaxed. They might run over the other team.

No matter what, I never worried about the Raiders not being up for the Monday night game with that big national audience. Great players like to show off. Monday night they had the biggest possible stage to show off on.

In a big game, Ken Stabler and George Blanda wanted to pass on every play. Fred Biletnikoff wanted a pass thrown to him on every play. Mark Van Eeghen, Marv Hubbard, Clarence Davis, and Pete Banaszak wanted to run the ball on every play. Art Shell and Gene Upshaw wanted every rushing play run to their side. Ted Hendricks wanted to make the tackle on every play. Willie Brown wanted to knock down every pass. Those guys wanted the pressure. They wanted the big audience. That's what made them so great. Especially on Monday night.

"The whole world's watching," I always reminded them.

That's all they had to hear. They loved it. In my nine seasons of Monday night games, beginning in 1970 with the NFL realignment, the Raiders had an 11–1–1 record, the best of any team in that span. It wasn't an accident. We had great players on that great stage.

Great players all have the same five ingredients—toughness, aggressiveness in making the big play, pride, knowledge, and dedication.

Toughness. At the Pro Bowl once, I was sitting around with some of my AFC players when Larry Csonka defined toughness. "It's doing what you have to do to get the job done," he said, "even though you don't enjoy it. And doing it with the same enthusiasm you have for those things you do enjoy." Like when a great deep receiver works hard on catching short passes.

Aggressiveness in making the big play. Have you ever noticed how the same guys keep making almost all the big plays?

Pride. People with pride make a commitment to be the best, to win all their games, to lead the league. For those people, fear of failure is the greatest motivator. Their pride pushes against that fear. Without pride, fear of failure is just fear. At the Pro Bowl after O.J. Simpson rushed for a record 2,003 in the 1973 season, I noticed in our locker room before the game that he couldn't sit still.

"Is this game that big to you?" I asked.

"Every game is that big," O.J. said. "I don't want to be *one* of the best. I want to be the *best* of the best."

"That's why you are the best of the best," I said.

Knowledge. Every great player knows not only what he does on a play, but he also knows what everybody on the team is supposed to do. Any time a tackle tells me, "I'm the tackle, I don't know what the guard does," I'm not impressed. If the tackle doesn't know what the guard does, then he really doesn't know what *he* does. It's the same way in business. When a salesman tells me, "I don't know how this thing works, I just sell it," I look for a salesman who does know how it works.

Dedication. When a great player keeps messing up a play for one reason or another, he'll keep asking for one more shot at it. He'll keep working until he gets it right. The average player won't bother.

"I've done mine," he'll say.

That's why he's average. It's the same with successful coaches. I never knew where I was going to learn something that would help me. On a flight from San Francisco to New Orleans to coach the Pro Bowl after the 1975 season, a stewardess tapped me on the shoulder.

"Jack Nicklaus wants to say hello," she said. "He has an empty seat next to him."

Our flight went on to Miami after stopping in New Orleans, so Jack was on his way home to North Palm Beach, Florida, where he's a big Dolphin fan. That season the Dolphins had beaten us, 27–10, in the AFC championship game in Miami. We talked football awhile; then I had a question.

"What makes the difference in golfers?" I said.

"What do you mean by the difference?" he said.

"All those guys on the PGA Tour have to be good golfers," I said. "But what's the difference in them? Why do you and a few other guys win a lot of tournaments? Why do some guys only win once in a while? Why do some guys never win?"

"Practice," he said.

I had been expecting him to answer guts or nerve, or whatever you want to call it when a golfer has to make a six-foot putt.

"Practice?" I said.

"Knowing how to practice," Jack said. "Most people think I'm practicing before I play, but I'm not. I'm just warming up. I practice after the round. The first thing I practice is every shot that I hit poorly that day. Then I practice all the shots I didn't have to hit that day. If on Sunday you have to hit a three-iron, for example, and you haven't hit a three-iron during the three previous rounds of the tournament, you're not too sure of yourself. But if you've hit your three-iron in practice every day, you're confident of hitting it well.

"All golfers like to practice the shots they hit well. Conversely, not enough practice the shots they don't hit well. As a result, they don't get any better.

"Ever since I learned that, I not only became a better golfer, but I slept better," Jack said, laughing. "Before that, I could never get to sleep. I would be thinking about all the shots I had missed. If I hit a seven-iron poorly, it would keep me awake. But by practicing a seven-iron after the round until I was hitting it well, I went right to sleep."

"That's the same with me," I said. "When I started using a tape recorder to put down everything I wanted to do the next day instead of thinking about it after I went to bed, I went right to sleep, too. The next morning, it's there."

We had such a good conversation, when our plane landed in New Orleans, I almost forgot to get off. The next season, I translated what Jack had talked about into what I could use as a coach. I put up a checklist of everything the players had to do each day. That way, nothing was new to them on Sunday if we had to do it. As for me, I kept talking into my tape recorder on the twenty-five-minute drive home from practice. In the car, I'd tape everything we had to do the next day. Maybe a new play, maybe something I wanted to say to the team or to one of the players. The next morning, I'd turn on the tape recorder, play it back, and take it from there.

By this time, I was lecturing at coaching clinics, not just listening as I had as a young coach. At a Philadelphia clinic once, I talked about how I used a tape recorder.

Years later, I was with Dick Vermeil, then the Eagles' coach. He told me how the week before a game he would tape his thoughts about the offensive game plan. On Saturday, he would give the tape to his quarterbacks for them to listen to that night.

"That's a good idea," I said.

"You know who I learned that from?" he asked.

"Who?"

"You."

He had sat in on my lecture at that Philadelphia clinic years before. That, too, is coaching—a handing down of ideas. Jack Nicklaus, of all people, had influenced me and then I had influenced Dick Vermeil and in the future I'm sure Dick will influence other coaches. That will go on and on.

5

My Friend Al Davis

WE HAD JUST LOST THE 1975 AFC CHAMPI-
onship game to the Steelers, 16–10, a tough
game on a tough afternoon in Pittsburgh—
cold, bitter, gray. I talked to my team in our dressing
room at Three Rivers Stadium, then I walked over to
a side room to talk to the writers. I had answered a
few questions when a strange voice spoke up.

"Al," he said, "why did you?..."

"My name's John," I said. "That's a helluva thing at
this point."

"Sorry," he said.

I was finishing my seventh year as the Raiders'
coach, five times in the AFC championship game, in
the playoffs every season except one. But one guy still
thought I was Al Davis, which meant he must never
have seen a picture of Al or me. Al is slim, with slicked-
back hair, and anytime it's the least bit cold he wears
a trenchcoat. I'm not exactly slim, I have a hairdo like

a mop, and if it's chilly, I wear a windbreaker. Other than that, there's no difference. Except that Al is the Raiders' owner, the managing general partner. I worked for Al, which some people thought had to be a problem. But it never was.

In other cities around the NFL, some sportswriters believed that I was Al's puppet, that Al was pulling the strings. Hey, he needed ropes to pull me, anyway. But in the Oakland area, the writers knew I was the coach.

Al came to practice but he always stayed down near the end zone. Never out on the field. Never anywhere near the huddle. Any writers who were there knew I was the coach. More important, I knew my players knew I was the coach. Not that I didn't listen to Al when he talked football. Al knows football. But he never "interfered" with me like some people assumed. In my ten years as the Raider coach, Al and I had a great relationship.

Al and I didn't just work together. We were, and are, the best of friends.

I really got to know Al at—of all places—baseball games. In the Raider offices in May and June, the phone was always ringing, visitors were always dropping in. Al and I never had much time to talk. But whenever the Oakland A's were playing a weekday night game, Al and I would go over to the Coliseum and sit up in the Raider box on the press level. With no phone and no visitors, we talked about trades, players—anything and everything. It got so that if I had something important to discuss with Al at that time of year, I always waited until we went to the A's game. After four or five innings, we'd go over to Vince's restaurant for dinner.

Every year before training camp, Al and I took our

wives to Las Vegas to relax for a few days. That trip always coincided with his birthday, July 4.

Al doesn't gamble, he doesn't drink, he hardly ever went to any of the Vegas shows. But he loved to sit out in the sun by the pool. That relaxed him.

Al had turned the Raiders around in his three seasons as coach before I was hired as an assistant. He changed the colors to silver and black. He coined the Raider motto—"pride and poise." He started calling the Raiders "the dynamic organization" with a "commitment to excellence." In the week before the Raiders won Super Bowl XVIII in Tampa, silver-and-black billboards with "commitment to excellence" were all over town. Maybe it's corny but Al's three Super Bowl rings justify that phrase. I'm not a big numbers guy but from the time Al took over the Raiders in 1963 through Super Bowl XVIII, the Raiders have had a .709 winning percentage (225 wins, 92 losses, 11 ties), the best record in major-league sports during that span. Better than the Montreal Canadiens in hockey, the Boston Celtics in basketball, and the Baltimore Orioles in baseball. Of the 28 NFL teams, the Raiders have had the best overall regular-season record since 1960—215 wins, 115 losses and 11 ties for a .652 percentage. (Next are the Dallas Cowboys at .643 and the Miami Dolphins at .621.)

Over nearly a quarter of a century, the coaches and the players have changed but Al Davis has remained the Raiders' constant—at first the general manager and coach, and from 1966 the managing general partner.

Not long after I joined the Raiders in 1967 as a linebacker coach, I heard the story that typifies what Al is all about. In those years, Tom Flores, now the

Raiders' coach, was Al's quarterback. During a game Tom limped to the bench with a shoulder injury. George Anderson, the Raider trainer, quickly taped an ice bag to the shoulder. But when Tom stayed on the bench, Al stared at George.

"C'mon, c'mon," Al said impatiently, "is that the coldest ice you've got?"

Al was named the AFL Commissioner in 1966 but after he helped force the merger with the NFL a few months later, he returned to the Raiders as managing general partner. Al knew football from a coach's standpoint, which made it easier for me to deal with him— not harder as some people thought. Al was also the only boss I had to answer to, which also made it easier, not harder.

To me, the best job for a coach is where he's his own boss. Paul Brown, Vince Lombardi, and George Halas had that situation, but not many others have.

I've always felt sorry for a coach with several names above his on the Club Directory in the media guide— chairman, president, executive vice-president, general manager. Almost anytime a club has that many bosses, the coach doesn't have a chance. Sooner or later one of those bosses is going to want a new coach. But from the moment Al promoted me to head coach in 1969, he was my only boss. I didn't need to check with a committee or go to board meetings. I just went to Al— not that we always agreed.

"I've had fights with John; we have disagreed from the very first day," Al once was quoted. "That's why I like him."

And that's why I liked *him*. When you're a coach, you need someone to bounce your ideas off, just as he enjoyed bouncing his ideas off me.

Al was born in Brockton, Massachusetts, grew up in Brooklyn, and went to Syracuse University, but he developed a semi-Southern accent in the 50's at Fort Belvoir, Virginia, as the head coach of an Army team and later at The Citadel in Charleston, South Carolina, as an assistant coach. But I never had any trouble understanding him, especially when he was bouncing an idea off me.

"What about Stabler?" he once said to me. "Do you think it's time we traded Stabler?"

I didn't even answer Al that time. If the Raiders had traded Ken Stabler in those years, they might as well have traded me. Al knew I felt that way. He was just testing me, making sure I still felt that way. Al believes that if you don't believe in something strong enough to fight for it, then you don't believe in it strong enough to do it. Al always would make you stick up for what you believed. Not because he didn't agree with you, but just to see if you felt strongly—especially about a possible trade.

Al never made a trade without talking to me about it. In my ten years as head coach, I agreed on every trade we made. But there was one trade I didn't feel right about. I don't think Al felt right about it either. When we needed a defensive lineman in 1972, we traded Raymond Chester, the All-AFC tight end the previous season, to the Colts for Bubba Smith, who was coming off knee surgery. Bubba was never the same Bubba for us that he had been before he got a leg tangled in the chain of a first-down marker. But we had been searching for a defensive end for so long, Al and I figured if we didn't take a gamble on Bubba, we might never get one.

I argued against trading Raymond for Bubba, but

I didn't argue that we had to gamble on a defensive lineman. At the time, defensive linemen were at a premium much more than now. In the four-man defensive line every team used then, a good pass-rushing end could dominate a game.

Al always enjoyed judging player personnel, especially college players in all-star games. In the days before the 1974 East–West game, Al went over to Palo Alto to watch the two squads work out. But when it rained hard that afternoon, I assumed it had been a wasted trip. I was still in my office when Al walked in.

"John," he said, "I found your next fullback."

"What fullback? Who are you talking about?"

"Mark Van Eeghen, the kid from Colgate—he can play, John, he's a player."

"Where did you see him?"

"I watched him work out."

"Did they work out in all that rain?" I said.

"No, in the gym."

"In the gym? What were they wearing?"

"Shorts and sneakers."

"You know he's a player from seeing him in the gym?"

"He did some things I liked."

"What could he do in the gym?"

"The way he moved, the way he held his hands. This kid can play, John, he's a player. He's your next fullback."

"You sure?"

"I'm sure."

In the draft a few weeks later we took Mark Van Eeghen in the third round. At the time our starting fullback, Marv Hubbard, was from Colgate, so some people thought we just took another Colgate fullback. But that had nothing to do with why Al liked him. Over the next eight seasons, Mark rushed for 5,907 yards, caught 162 passes for 1,467 yards and scored 38 touchdowns. Al had discovered the Raiders' all-time rushing leader in a gym wearing shorts and sneakers.

"I can watch a guy for ten seconds," Al liked to say, "and tell if he's a player."

If horse racing were Al's business, he would love those yearling auctions where they walk each horse out for everybody to see them. Al would pick more stakes winners than anybody else. Al might even find a way to talk to the horse. People in the NFL always think that Al will find a way to do anything, even move a franchise without permission. Because of his reputation, whenever the Raiders were involved in anything controversial, Al got the blame. Which kept the blame off me. Anytime a helicopter flew over another team's practice field during the week, their coach assumed that Al had a spy up there. I've heard that when Harland Svare was coaching the Chargers, he was sitting in the visiting team's locker room at the Oakland Coliseum, staring up at the light fixture.

"Damn you, Al Davis, damn you," he said. "I know you're up there, Al Davis, damn you."

Harland apparently thought that Al had planted a listening device in the light fixture. Leave it to Al to let Harland stew. When he was told about Harland's outburst, Al shrugged.

"The thing," he said, "wasn't in the light fixture, I'll tell you that."

The day before the 1968 AFL championship game with the Jets, we practiced at Shea Stadium in a freezing bitter wind. Trying to stay warm, Dick Romanski, our equipment man, was talking to a friend of Harry Schuh, one of our offensive tackles. Harry's friend was in the plastics business. When we went on the field Sunday for the warmup, Dick and Harry's friend had rigged up what looked like a plastic chicken coop around our bench.

As soon as Milt Woodard, the AFL president, saw the plastic coop, he ordered it removed. Milt blamed Al, but Dick Romanski and Harry Schuh's friend were the only ones who knew about the coop. Al didn't know about it until he saw it.

We lost the title game to the Jets, 27–23, but Al soon had another surprise after we returned to Oakland. All the assistant coaches were sitting around the office one day, rating the college players for the draft, when John Rauch, the Raiders' head coach for three seasons, suddenly walked in and closed the door.

"I'm leaving," John announced. "I'm taking the Buffalo job. If any of you want to be on my staff there, you've got a job."

Whenever any team's head coach leaves, his assistants usually have heard the whispers. But none of us had heard anything about the possibility of John leaving the Raiders, not a word. In the papers the next day, John was quoted as complaining about Al.

"We couldn't get along," John was quoted. "Al wouldn't let me be myself; a lot of people said it was his team. Well, it wasn't."

I don't know about John, but I know the assistant coaches didn't see much of Al that season. Al was in the office in Oakland while we were out in Hayward, where we practiced then. Every so often John would complain that Al was doing this or that, but we never saw it. One time we put a defensive coverage into a game plan late in the week at a meeting with John and the assistant coaches involved with defense—Tom Dahms, Charlie Sumner, and me. The next day John was reading through the game plan.

"Where did this coverage come from?" he asked.

"That's the coverage we put in last night," I said.

"No, we didn't."

"Yes, we did," I said.

"No, no, Davis put that in."

"We did it last night, John."

"The hell we did."

"Hey, listen, John, don't you remember..." Charlie said, recreating the discussion we had the night before.

"Oh, yeah," John said, "I remember now."

As far as I know, Al never told any of the assistant coaches to put a coverage or a play or anything else into the game plan. But the day John told us he was leaving, all the assistants were still staring at each other a few minutes later when Al walked in. He sounded as surprised as we had been.

"This is a shock," Al said, "but you all have a job next season if you want to stay. After the draft, if anyone here thinks he should be the head coach, I'll talk to you about it."

In the next few days, the Steelers hired Chuck Noll as their new head coach. That season Chuck had been an assistant under Don Shula with the Colts, but we had gotten to know each other in San Diego back when he was an assistant with the Chargers and I was an assistant at San Diego State. After I joined the Raiders in 1967, we arranged to take our spring college scouting trips together. We were good friends then, real good friends. The day after Chuck took the Steeler job, he phoned me.

"John," he said, "I want you to be my defensive coordinator."

"Hey, thanks, Chuck, thanks a lot," I told him, "but I want to stay in Oakland and take my chances on the head job here."

"You're the first guy I've called about this job," Chuck said, "but I don't know how long I can wait to fill it."

"I'm not asking you to wait," I answered. "I'll take my chances."

Now that I look back on what happened, if the Steelers hadn't hired Chuck first, Al might have hired him as the Raiders' head coach. Al was close to Chuck, too. Al had been an assistant coach with the Chargers when Chuck was an assistant. But now Chuck was no longer a candidate. The day I told Al that I was interested in being the Raiders' coach, he invited me into his office. It's decorated in black and silver, naturally. At thirty-two, I knew I was young to be a head coach in the NFL, but I thought I was ready.

"I don't have any head-coaching experience in the NFL," I told him, "but if I don't get this job, I'm not going to have any head-coaching experience three years from now or five years from now."

Al knew me only as an assistant coach on defense, so he asked me about my thoughts on offense. I told him that I had always believed in knowing the whole picture, not just defense or offense. Even though I had been coaching our linebackers, I had always tried to know as much as possible about our offensive game plan. And, naturally, about the offenses of all the teams we played.

"You can't defend anybody," I said, "if you don't know their offensive philosophy."

"If you get this job," Al said to me, "what do you think your strengths would be?"

"Defense—and dealing with people," I replied. "I think I know how to deal with people."

"I'll tell you what," Al said. "Let's see, this is Thursday—I'll call you Sunday."

I had no idea where I stood. I thought I had come off all right with Al, but it was hard to tell. And by this time, some of the local newspapers had begun to speculate. One of the San Francisco papers was predicting that Ollie Spencer, who had been the offensive line coach for seven seasons, would get the head job. None of the Bay Area papers were talking about me. But on Saturday, a friend phoned me at my Pleasanton home.

"Have you seen the *San Mateo Times*?" he asked.

"No, we don't get the San Mateo paper here."

"Ron Reid wrote that you're going to get the job. Have you heard anything from Al yet?"

"Not a word," I said.

"You better get the *Times* and see what Reid wrote."

I put Virginia and the boys in the car and drove across the bridge to San Mateo on the other side of the bay. I opened the *Times* to the sports page and there was Ron's story—"Madden Next Raider Coach."

"Don't get too excited," Virginia cautioned. "You're not the coach until Al tells you that you're the coach."

Al told me he would phone the next day, Sunday, either way. But driving back to Pleasanton, it occurred to me that Al might phone when I'd be with Virginia and the boys at mass. As we talked about it, I had the solution.

"Let's get our baby-sitter, Michelle, for the morning," I said.

"What do we need a baby-sitter for Sunday morning?" Virginia said. "We always take the boys to church with us Sunday morning."

"Not for the boys," I explained. "For the phone."

I was awake early that Sunday, waiting for the phone to ring. Hour after hour, nothing. When it was time for us to go to late mass, Michelle arrived. I explained to her why we needed her.

"It's a very important call," I said.

When we returned from mass, Al still hadn't phoned. But early in the afternoon he did.

"Meet me at the Edgewater," he said.

He gave me the number of the room he had taken at what is now the Edgewater Hyatt House, a motel that was near the Raider offices.

"Don't go through the lobby," Al said. "Park in the back."

I liked the secrecy. I figured Al wouldn't be so concerned about somebody seeing me unless he was going to offer me the job. After we talked awhile, he did. "You can tell Virginia," he said, "but I want you to hide until Tuesday's press conference."

"Hide?"

"Yeah," he said. "If you go home and a newspaperman happens to call and ask you what's happening, then you won't have to lie. Find an out-of-the-way place, let me know where you are, and stay in your room there until Tuesday morning. The only person I want you to go see is Ollie Spencer, so he hears it from you as well as me. Ollie was here before I was. He deserves to know the situation before we announce it. And think about what you're going to say at the press conference."

"I'll call you," I said, "and I'll see Ollie."

I drove home, gave Virginia the news, packed a little

bag, drove to the Fremont Inn and checked in. I phoned Al to let him know where I was if he needed me, then I drove to Ollie's house. Ollie had wanted the job as much as I did but he told me he would help me all he could. After that I went back to my room at the Fremont Inn, watched TV, read the newspapers, ordered room service, and thought about how I would answer the questions at the press conference. I knew one question would be how I would co-exist with Al, and I had my answer ready.

"I'd be a fool not to listen to Al Davis," I said when the time came, "but when we're in combat, the decisions have to be mine."

I was big news that day, but not as big as I thought I might be. On page one of the *Oakland Tribune*, one headline covered two pro football stories:

"RAIDERS NAME COACH
PACKERS LOSE LOMBARDI."

That same day, Vince Lombardi had announced that he was resigning as the Packers' general manager (he had stopped coaching a year earlier) in order to join the Redskins as their general manager and coach. What hurt even more was that Lombardi's name was in the *Tribune* headline, but mine wasn't. And Virginia told me how the boys had reacted when she informed them that they would be able to see their daddy on the TV news that night. (Mike was five then, Joe was three.)

"I want to watch 'Batman,'" Mike told her.

"Me too," Joe said. "Batman and Robin."

At the press conference, Al Davis talked about how he disagreed with Vince Lombardi's claim that creating a championship football team is a team's biggest challenge. "The biggest challenge," Al said, "is maintaining, and that's John's challenge now—maintaining our team at its high level and going forward from there." That challenge didn't bother me. If it had, I wouldn't have wanted the job. But nobody helped me maintain the Raiders at a high level more than Al did. My first year as coach, Al realized that I was worrying too much about the little things, such as the last few players on the roster.

"Just remember this," he told me one day, "your name is at the top of the coaching staff. You're the head coach. It doesn't make a goddam bit of difference what other people think. All that counts is what you do."

I never forgot that. Even now in TV, it's what I do and what I say. I can't worry about hurting somebody's feelings. I have to do and to say what I think is the right thing, not what other people think is the right thing. Just by saying that, Al made it easier for me to be a head coach. Al also made it easier another way.

"All you have to do," he told me, "is coach the team. Nothing else. Except the Friday before every home game, you have to attend the Raider booster-club luncheon. These people in the booster club were the first to help me when I came here. We don't really need them anymore but they were there when we *did* need them."

Other than that, I didn't have to make any appearances unless I wanted to. I made a few, but not many. I didn't have a TV show, I didn't have a radio show. Without these side deals that some coaches have, I just zeroed in on one job—coaching.

Right after I took over, I went to Al with an idea.

In addition to bringing in our rookies for a weekend, I wanted to bring in the rookies for what are known now as minicamps. All the teams do it now, but I don't think any team was doing it then. I didn't know how Al would react to that. Housing and feeding the players adds up fast, but Al never blinked.

"That sounds great," he said. "Let's do that."

I wanted the players to practice, but I also wanted to practice myself. Practice being a head coach. I didn't want to go to training camp in July and stand out there wondering what I was supposed to be doing. Our three rookie minicamps that year were real camps. Other teams might bring in players for physical exams and put them on a weight-training program. But at our minicamp we played football. With pads. With films. By the time we went to Santa Rosa to open our real training camp, I had an idea of what it was like to be a head coach. And when we were looking at our schedule, I suggested to Al that on trips to the East we leave a day earlier than usual in order to practice there and get acclimated.

"Good idea," he said.

When all the coaches were having trouble sharing five movie projectors, I suggested to Al that we get twenty projectors.

"Good idea," he said again.

On some clubs, a business manager might turn down requests like that. Too expensive. But with Al, anything that helped the football team was automatically okayed. Al is a football man first, then a businessman. I also figured Al wouldn't mind having a new projector to watch game films. His devotion to the team is the reason he has seldom had a contract problem with a player. Whenever one of our best players deserved a new contract, Al usually gave it to him before the player asked. I never knew what the players' salaries were. I didn't want to know. But one year when Al signed guard Gene Upshaw for, let's say, $100,000, he gave offensive tackle Art Shell a new contract for $100,000, too —long before Art's contract expired. Al did that with several players. In my ten years I don't ever remember having a player who didn't want to play because of a contract problem.

"You've got to pay the players," Al always said.

Al has also believed in keeping Raider players in the organization. When the Raiders won Super Bowl XVIII, seven former Raiders were either coaches or scouts—head coach Tom Flores, assistant coaches Willie Brown, Art Shell, and Terry Robiskie; scouts Dan Conners, Kent McCloughan, and Bob Mischak.

Tom Flores has done a great job as my successor— two Super Bowl rings in his first five seasons. Tom had been the receivers' coach on my staff for seven seasons. Earlier he had been the Raiders' quarterback the first seven seasons of the franchise. That's when Al got to know him. I was hoping Al would name him, but Al never asked me for a recommendation. That was his decision to make.

Years before I had learned not to get involved in Al's decisions. In the 1973 draft we took John Vella out of Southern Cal, a 6'4", 255-pound All-American offensive tackle. I had gone down to SC to look at some of their players. I had really liked John and I told him so.

"Too bad you won't be there by the time we draft," I said.

But as the draft progressed, Vella was still there. We took him in the second round. When the writers asked me about him, I told them what a great prospect he was—and then I made my mistake.

"He should've been a first-round pick," I said.

When that line appeared in the papers the next day, Al knew that Vella's agent would see it and ask for a contract worthy of a first-round choice, not a second-round choice. Which is exactly what happened.

"John," he told me, "never praise a draft choice too much until he's signed."

Al was always aware of the money. That's why he moved the Raiders from Oakland to Los Angeles before the 1982 season. I've always thought that Los Angeles didn't steal the Raiders as much as Oakland let them get away. Al wanted luxury boxes in the Oakland Coliseum as an extra source of income. In the NFL, the home team splits the game receipts with the visiting team on a sixty–forty basis—except for the income from luxury boxes. The home team keeps all that money. Around that same time, the Los Angeles Coliseum people knew the Rams were moving down the freeway to Anaheim Stadium in 1980, so Al started talking about building luxury boxes in the L.A. Coliseum if the Raiders moved there.

Another factor in the move was that the Raiders' lease in Oakland was up. Al didn't break his lease, he didn't break his contract. He had, so to speak, played out his option. Al's argument was, "I'm not going to lease the Oakland Coliseum for the future unless it's a stadium for the future—with luxury boxes." But for all the controversy that boiled in those years, I think Al wanted to keep the Raiders in Oakland if a suitable arrangement could be worked out. The week before Super Bowl XIV, I was in the lobby of the Beverly

Wilshire in Los Angeles when Al saw me. He hurried over.

"We're going to stay in Oakland," he told me. "I just met with Mayor Wilson and Cornell Maier; it's going to work out."

Mayor Lionel Wilson of Oakland and Cornell Maier, the chairman of Kaiser Aluminum, were representing the city, but the deal collapsed when they couldn't get it approved by all the other Oakland and Alameda politicians. That was the primary problem—too many different people were involved in the decision.

With the Raiders, it was simple. Al ran the club. I ran the team. Ron Wolf ran the scouting. Al LoCasale ran the office. I didn't even have a secretary. I used Al's. That's how simple it was to work with Al—not for Al, *with* Al.

In my ten years as head coach, we never had a serious conflict about anything. Well, one thing. Al always thought that you built a team with cornerbacks and I always thought you built a team with offensive linemen.

"Cornerbacks," he would say. "You start with cornerbacks."

"No, no," I would say. "You start with offensive linemen."

We argued that for ten years, but it never developed into a serious difference of opinion for a very simple reason. I agreed that cornerbacks were the second most important position in building a team and Al agreed that offensive linemen were second. We got along because we had that kind of respect for each other's opinion and for each other. After we won Super Bowl XI, a New York attorney named Marty Blackman approached Al one day about maybe doing a TV commercial.

"I don't want to do that stuff," Al told him. "But you know who you ought to get a commercial for?"

"Who?" Marty asked.

"My coach," Al said.

6

**Breaking
Through**

IT DIDN'T HAPPEN RIGHT AWAY. AND IT CAME CLOSE to never happening at all. Marty Blackman, the New York attorney who is also the casting director for the Miller Lite commercials, phoned me early in 1978, but I wasn't interested. I was still coaching then, still wrapped up in football. Marty phoned again early in 1979 after I had decided to stop coaching, but I still wasn't that interested.

"No, not me," I told him. "I just want to relax."

"But it's easy," he said, "and the money is good."

I don't even remember how much money Marty mentioned and at the time I didn't care. I just didn't want to be bothered. I was doing some speaking engagements for Hewlett-Packard and IBM, but I guess Marty thought I was trying to hold up Miller for more money.

"Think about it," he said. "I'll get back to you."

The next time Marty phoned, I still wasn't too sure

I wanted to do it but I had begun to get a little restless sitting around the house. He told me that the producers of the Miller Lite commercials were going to be in Los Angeles in April.

"Instead of coming to New York," he explained, "you could do the audition in L.A."

The audition was important because the Miller Lite executives in Milwaukee always want to see how the idea looks on tape before they commit themselves to a commercial. I still wasn't sure, but Marty's timing had been perfect. I had to be in L.A. anyway for a speaking engagement when the Miller Lite producers would be there. So I figured, what the hell, maybe I'll flunk the audition and that'll be the end of it.

"All right," I said, "I'll do the audition in L.A."

I went to a little Hollywood studio and blinked at those big lights. I talked about how "I'm not the same crazy coach who used to storm around the sidelines yelling at the officials," then I went home and forgot about it. Two weeks later, my phone rang.

"They loved the audition," Marty said. "Can you come to New York in June to shoot the commercial?"

The trip to New York appealed to me more than the commercial. At the time I was still flying but for years I had promised my boys to take them across the country by train. This was the ideal opportunity. We boarded the California Zephyr in Martinez, just outside Oakland, rode it all the way to Chicago, then changed to the Lake Shore Limited and eventually rolled into Grand Central Terminal. The next day we went over to Caliban's, a bar at Third Avenue and East 26th Street where the commercial would be shot.

One thing about the Miller Lite commercials, they are shot in real places, not on a set. Backer & Spielvogel, the advertising agency, rents a real bar for a day. Or a bowling alley or a softball field. For me once, they even rented an Amtrak train that went all the way from Penn Station to Philadelphia and back.

In my first commercial, the advertising people had a new ending to what I had done in the audition. Actually, they had two endings—one with me breaking through a paper wall, waving my arms, as crazy as ever; one without the paper. Bob Giraldi, the director, and Nick Gisonde, the art director, thought that the version with me breaking through the paper might be more violent than funny, that it might scare the viewer instead of sell the viewer. To be safe, they shot the two different endings. But when the Miller Lite people in Milwaukee saw them, they liked the one with me breaking through the paper. I'm glad they did. Along with my work at CBS, breaking through that paper for Miller Lite made me more famous than I ever was as a coach.

"You won't believe the recognition you'll get out of this," Marty Blackman had told me. "It's fantastic."

I was skeptical. I had been on TV in the Super Bowl, in all those championship and playoff games, in Monday night games. I knew what it was like to be recognized from national television—especially when you're as big a guy as I am—but Marty was right. Wherever I go now, strangers come up to me, repeat that line about how "I'm not the same crazy coach," and wave their arms. It's fun.

"You know him, Myrtle," I hear men saying to their wives. "He's the one in the beer commercial, the one who breaks through the paper."

I'm a people-person. When people relate to me, I relate to them. Kids who never saw me coach will yell,

"Tastes great!" I yell back, "Less Filling!" (With my bulk, the less filling the better.) I like Miller Lite, but some people expect me always to have a Lite in my hand. I was having breakfast once when a stranger stared at me.

"Where's your Miller Lite?" he said.

"Hey, it's eight o'clock in the morning," I answered. "Do you drink beer for breakfast?"

"Of course not."

"I don't either."

I did that first commercial in thirty takes, which I thought was a lot, but it turned out to be a record. It's taken some guys sixty or seventy to get it just the way the producers and directors want. When my boys and I returned home, Dave Newhouse, the sports columnist for the *Oakland Tribune*, interviewed me about making the commercial. I told him about the thirty takes and he mentioned it in his column. Billy Martin was managing the Oakland A's then and apparently he read Dave's column. The next time I saw Billy, he got all over me.

"The commercial I did with George Steinbrenner," he said, "we had less than thirty takes."

"That's not what they told me," I shot back, letting him take the bait. "I guess you're just a little slower than I am, Billy; you need a little more time to do it right."

"You got some nerve," Billy said, "putting me down in *my* town."

Billy had grown up in Berkeley, right next to Oakland, but after all my years with the Raiders, I thought Oakland was my town too. Suddenly we had a friendly feud going.

"My next commercial," Billy said, "I won't need thirty takes."

His next commercial, Billy was a cowboy in a black hat standing at the bar with his back to Jim Shoulders, the rodeo cowboy. Near the end, Jim says, "You see, you don't wanna get filled up when you're out there punching doggies." Then he turns, says, "Ain't that right, cowboy?" and taps Billy on the shoulder.

"I didn't punch that doggie," Billy says.

I happened to be in New York the day they were shooting that commercial at City Limits, a bar on the Lower East Side, so I dropped by. After about thirty takes, they weren't anywhere near finished.

"Stick with it, Billy," I said. "See ya later."

I had fun needling Billy, but the number of takes doesn't necessarily mean you're good or bad at making a commercial. "That's excellent," Bob Giraldi likes to say, "but make it better this time." They do another take. And another. And another. You can say your lines perfectly each time, but Bob will like your expression or your attitude in one better than in another. Or he won't like the reaction of the people in the background, the extras. One of those guys might have smiled when he should have frowned. Those extras are professional actors. Sometimes they overact and Bob has to remind them to cool it. Bob doesn't have that trouble with me or the other Miller Lite guys. He knows we're not actors. We're not even supposed to memorize our lines. If we did, Bob knows the words would sound like we memorized them—stiff. Instead, he wants us to be ourselves in whatever situation the commercial calls for.

"Pretend," he told me one time, "the Raiders just lost with two seconds to go."

When the commercial has Rodney Dangerfield in it, Bob wants us to think of Rodney as a jerk, a klutz. Bob doesn't want us to chirp, "Oh...no...not Rodney" like we were in the third grade. He wants us to put on sour faces and grunt, "Ah, no, not Rodney!" like he is the last guy we want to be bowling with the match at stake, or the last guy we want to bring in as a relief pitcher to a softball game. In our bowling commercial, Rodney has to walk through a bunch of us to get to the alley. When we taped it, some of us decided not to let Rodney through. Rodney was standing to the side waiting for his cue, all pumped up, but Bubba Smith, Dick Butkus, Tom Heinsohn, Deacon Jones, and I just stood there like a wall. Rodney couldn't even see over us, much less get through us.

"You guys," he grumbled. "I knew you were going to do this to me."

For all the egos involved, the Miller Lite guys really get along great. Nobody tries to upstage the others. The reason for that, I think, is that our personalities are pretty much the same: we're competitors and we're hams. When you think about it, Mickey Spillane the author isn't that much different from Billy Martin the manager. Tom Heinsohn the basketball player isn't that much different from Dick Butkus the football player. The only one who's different, quite obviously, is Lee Meredith, the blonde Mickey Spillane calls "Doll," the only woman in the commercials. Lee's a great gal. She has to take a lot from all the guys, more off-camera than on-camera.

But nobody has to take as much as Bubba Smith, who has a way of asking for it.

In our boardroom commercial to determine who's the "most popular" of the Miller Lite spokesmen, several of us speak up on our own behalf, including me, then Mickey Spillane asks for a secret ballot. At the lectern, Rodney declares, "Gentlemen, we have a winner," and then Bubba stands up, looks at a little slip of paper and announces defiantly, "Says here the winner is...Bubba Smith." But it wasn't quite as easy as that.

On the first take, Bubba stood up, looked at the paper and announced, "Says here the winner is...oh, shit." Bubba had forgotten his own name.

With that, everybody in the room got on Bubba, especially Billy Martin and Dick Butkus, who decided to make up a cue card for Bubba with his name on it. We don't ordinarily use cue cards. (Steve Horn, our director in that commercial, and Bob Giraldi consider cue cards artificial.) But as soon as Bubba stood up in the next take, Billy and Dick held up their cue card.

"Says here," Bubba said, "the winner is...Bubba Smith."

"Cut, cut," we heard Steve Horn say. "No, no, Bubba, you forgot to throw the piece of paper down."

"Oh, shit," Bubba said again.

At the table, Billy Martin grabbed another piece of paper and wrote another cue card with "throw paper" on it. The next take, Billy held up the card as Bubba stood up, announced, "Says here the winner is...Bubba Smith" and threw the paper up in the air.

"Cut, cut," Steve Horn said. "Bubba, you throw the paper *down*, not up."

By now, Bubba was steaming and sweating. At the table, Billy drew an arrow on the "throw paper" cue card.

"Down, the way the arrow is pointing," Billy said.

"Throw the paper *down* this time, Bubba, throw it *down!*"

Bubba finally got it right. To satisfy Bob, he had to do several more takes. It took us hours to do that commercial. For all his problems with his lines that day, Bubba is one of the few professional actors in the Miller Lite group. He's been in a couple of movies and on several TV shows. But that didn't stop Billy from pulling another prank on Bubba in our bowling-alley commercial. In that one, Dick Butkus picks up a bowling ball and says, "Hey, Bubba, this ball doesn't have any holes in it." Bubba grabs it, slams his fingers in it and says, "Now it does!" Actually the ball's three holes had been covered with black paper. But when it was time to do that scene, Billy substituted a regular ball. He had chalked what looked like three holes where the holes should be. He slipped that ball to Butkus, who would hand it to Bubba during the scene, but Butkus decided to double-cross Billy.

"Bubba, this is a bad ball," Dick whispered, "but don't let on."

With the camera rolling, Butkus handed him the ball—but Bubba forgot Dick's warning. Bubba tried to slam his fingers into what he thought were paper-covered holes, then he realized he had been had.

"Oh, shit," he said.

We all forget our lines, or forget what we're supposed to do, but Bubba sometimes forgets faces too. One day I was home when the phone rang. Marty Blackman was calling from where Bubba and Dick Butkus were doing their golf-course commercial.

"John, they want you to settle a bet," Marty said. "Is Cris Collinsworth white or black?"

At the time Cris was a rookie wide receiver with the

Cincinnati Bengals, who would play in Super Bowl XVI.

"He's white," I said.

"Are you sure?" Marty said.

"Yeah, I'm sure."

"That's what Butkus says too, but Bubba says that Collinsworth is black. They bet one hundred dollars and you're the arbiter. Whatever you say, that's it."

"He's white," I said.

In the background I heard Dick yelling, "I know Collinsworth is white, I met him," then I heard Bubba yelling, "I met him too, he's black," then I heard them both yelling.

"Bubba's refusing to pay," Marty said.

"I thought I was the arbiter," I said.

"You were until you said he's white!"

The week before the Super Bowl that season, Pat Summerall and I put every player on the Bengals and the 49ers on camera for our CBS interview spots. When we got to Cris, I told him about the bet and asked him to settle it.

"What can I tell you, Bubba," he said, staring into the camera, "I'm white."

Trouble seems to follow Bubba around. When we did our softball-game commercial, Bubba was running to second base when, wham, he crashed into Red Auerbach, whose cigar went one way and whose hat went the other. That same day, Boom-Boom Geoffrion was using a special softball glove with a big hole in it. When the ball went through it, smoke came out. The first take, Boom held the glove up in front of him instead of to the side. The ball flew through the hole and hit him in the gut.

"Next time," he said, wincing, "next time, I'll remember."

Next time. In our Miller Lite commercials, there are a lot of next times. And a lot of fun times. At the end of that softball commercial, I break through a paper billboard on the outfield fence, yelling, "Wait a minute, this game isn't over yet. I caught that ball." I had to do that scene a few times. After my last take, Billy Martin was standing out there near me.

"Put another paper billboard up there," Billy said to the workmen. "I want to try that."

Instead of just breaking through the paper legs-first, Billy dove through. He skinned his arms but he got up laughing. By now everybody was out there laughing, especially big Ben Davidson, who played defensive end on the Raiders for me.

"More paper," Ben called in his hoarse voice. "I want to do that."

"There's no more paper," one of the workmen said. "If you're going to break through the fence, you'll have to go through one of the wooden panels."

"What the hell, why not?" Ben said.

Without another word, Ben crashed through one of the wooden panels. He got up laughing and ran over to me.

"Hey, coach," he said, "remember when I did that?"

I remembered. At practice once, our defensive players were under orders not to tackle the ball-carrier, just touch him. Ben got so frustrated that on the last play of practice, he chased a ball-carrier all the way across the field, touched him, and kept on running toward the wooden fence that surrounded our practice field. Crash—he went right through the fence and took a whole panel of splintered wood with him.

"Remember that day in practice?" Ben was saying to me now after our commercial. "Remember that?"

They never change.

7

Character Study

THE DAY I ANNOUNCED MY RETIREMENT AS THE Raider coach, Ted Hendricks heard the news on the radio. But instead of phoning me, as most of my other players did, he drove over to Pleasanton to find me. Typical. Like most linebackers, Ted has to be where the action is. That's how he got his nickname. No, not "The Stork"—that's the nickname he got at the University of Miami because of his height. At 6'7", he was all legs then. On the Raiders he has another nickname that he got when he tried to jump over a pileup in a training-camp scrimmage. He didn't quite clear it. He accidentally kicked Marv Hubbard in the helmet, knocking him cold.

The other players began calling him "Kick-'em-in-the-Head Ted," which soon was shortened to just plain Kick-'em.

Only a few hours after he heard about my retirement, Kick-'em was sitting in the beer-and-wine bar

Virginia owned then over in Dublin, about a mile from our Pleasanton home. He was drinking beer the way he usually does —out of a pitcher instead of a glass. When he saw Virginia, he put down his pitcher.

"Where's John?" he asked.

"He's home," she said. "I just talked to him on the phone. He'll be home the rest of the afternoon. Drive over."

"Yeah, but I want to bring him a present."

"You know John," she said. "He doesn't want a present."

"No, I've got to bring him something."

"Just bring yourself, that's present enough."

"I'll think of something," he said.

When he arrived at the house, he walked in and handed me one of those big, red "Yield" traffic signs.

"Where did you get this?" I said.

"I stopped to see Virginia to find out what I should bring you," he said. "You know that right turn onto the road that goes over the Interstate, that's when I saw this sign. I said to myself, 'That's perfect.' I stopped the car, backed up and knocked the sign down. I put it in my car and here it is. Here's your present."

"Well, yeah," I said. "Thanks for the present, Ted."

The Yield sign is planted in our backyard now, but that day I put it in the kitchen, then I poured some Wild Turkey for Ted and me. We went into the family room and talked for a few hours, then he got up to leave.

"Thanks for the present," I said.

"It's a perfect present," he said.

Ted Hendricks was a free spirit long before it was fashionable to be a free spirit. When he joined the Raiders, he looked around and announced, "Everywhere I've been, I've been the screwball on the team—in college, with the Colts, with the Packers—but here I'm just a normal guy." In a way, he was right. We had more than our share of characters. But ol' Kick-'em seemed to be involved in more pranks than the others. One day in training camp at Santa Rosa, a kids' horse show was being held behind the fence of our practice field, but I wasn't paying any attention to it. At the start of practice, I walked out into the middle of the main field like I always did.

"All right," I yelled, "everybody up, let's go."

All the players trotted over and formed a circle around me. All but one. Suddenly a gate in the fence swung open and Ted rode into practice on a horse. I learned later that he had talked a little girl into letting him borrow her horse. From the grin on his face, I knew he expected me to go crazy—so I didn't. I let him ride up to where we were at midfield.

"That's nice, Ted," I said calmly. "Now get rid of the horse."

Another time, we were having our usual Friday special-teams meeting. For each unit, I always called out the position, then the proper player answered by calling out his name, then the backup at that position would call his name. I was going through the punt-return unit and as I yelled, "left end," our director of operations, Ron Wolf, leaned into the meeting room.

"John," he said seriously, "you've got an important phone call."

I hurried to the nearest phone, picked it up and heard, "Hendricks." As the left end on the punt-return unit, he was answering. Kick-'em is an original, not only as a character but as a player. Before he was drafted out of Miami (Florida) University, no NFL team knew where to play him. He had been an All-American defensive end, but he was only 215 pounds then. In projecting a player's future NFL position, coaches and scouts like to say, "This kid is like..." but Ted wasn't like anybody who had played in the NFL before. Ted was a new species. That's one reason he wasn't drafted until the second round, but Don Shula, then in his last year as the Colts' coach, found his position. Don put him at outside linebacker. Ted has been there ever since, an All-Pro in 1980 when the Raiders won Super Bowl XIV, a seven-time Pro Bowl selection, a member of four Super Bowl teams (three with the Raiders, one with the Colts).

Kick-'em was one of my favorite players. Now he's one of my favorite friends, along with Gene Upshaw, Art Shell, Dave Casper, Henry Lawrence, Ben Davidson, Dan Conners, and quite a few others who played for me.

Dan Conners was the Raiders' middle linebacker when I arrived as an assistant coach. On the field, he was all business, the quarterback of our defense. Off it, he was all fun. One time he needed a wrist operation. When the doctor showed him where the incision would be, Dan jumped.

"That'll ruin my career," he yelled.

"No, your wrist will be fine," the doctor said. "It'll be as good as new."

"No, my modeling career," he said. "I model wrist watches."

The doctor believed him. Instead of making the incision on top of the wrist, he did the operation underneath so the scar didn't show. Dan hasn't changed. Not long ago I saw him at a golf tournament where he got the booby prize for shooting 144.

"You should've cheated," I told him.

"I did cheat," he said. "I still shot 144!"

I never thought it was bad to let my players know I really like them. Once they knew that, it was easier to communicate with them. Knowing his coach likes him is more important to a player than anything else. To me, it was important to be able to chew out a player for screwing up and for him to accept it because he knew I liked him anyway. Some players actually like to be chewed out. One day during my first season as head coach, I had our quarterbacks wearing red jerseys, which meant not only do not tackle him, it meant *do not touch* any part of him, especially his arm. Quarterbacks get hurt often enough in a game without risking an injury in practice. But that day Ike Lassiter, one of our defensive ends, bumped into the arm of one of the quarterbacks.

"He's got a red jersey, Ike, he's *our* quarterback," I roared. "Hit the quarterback in the game, Ike, not in practice."

Two plays later Ben Davidson, our other defensive end, bumped a quarterback's arm. Only *two* plays before, he had heard me scream at Ike for the same thing. I hollered at Ben, too. I was still steaming when practice ended. I told one of the equipment men to tell Ben to see me in my office. When he arrived, I told him how I was more angry at him than I was at Ike, because he had heard me chew out Ike.

"Only two plays later," I said. "How could you do the same thing only two plays later?"

"You got mad at Ike," he said in that raspy voice, "and I wanted you to get mad at me."

Even at 6'8" and 280 pounds, Big Ben wanted to be noticed, whether it was doing something good or bad. That's why he grew his handlebar mustache, long before having a mustache was in. That's why he rode a motorcycle. More than any other player Ben created the image of the Raiders as Hell's Angels with shoulder pads, especially in 1967 when everybody thought he broke Joe Namath's cheekbone. In our next-to-last game that season Ben chased Namath over near the sideline and swatted him, his Jet helmet rolling along the grass as if he had been beheaded. X-rays later showed that Namath had a fractured cheekbone. Ben got the credit or the blame, depending on your point of view. But the next day, Ike Lassiter came in to complain.

"Ben didn't break Namath's cheekbone—I did," Ike said. "You'll see it in the films."

Sure enough, a few plays earlier, Namath got caught in a high-low. Somebody else had him by the legs when Ike whacked him high with an elbow. Not that it stopped Joe from finishing the game. Or the season. The following Sunday in San Diego, he wore a special mask while passing for 343 yards and a 14-game total of 4,007 yards—the first quarterback to surpass 4,000 yards in a season. It didn't stop him from anything else either. About three hours after his X-rays, he was seen checking out of the Edgewater in a tuxedo.

"We're off until Tuesday," Joe explained. "I'm going over to Vegas to have some fun."

Al Davis also had some fun. He had a photo blown up showing Big Ben standing over Namath, who is flying sideways with his helmet spinning in the air. Al put that blow-up on the wall of the stairway to the second floor of the Raider offices where everybody had to see it.

The twist to the story is that, off the field, Ben Davidson is one of the gentlest people I know. And one of the nicest. He's always appearing at charity functions. And, as a player, Ben got two free tickets to each Raider game, but he also bought twenty other tickets. I later found out that Ben went over to the Veterans Hospital and handed out those twenty tickets to patients. On him.

If he hadn't been so big, I don't think Ben would have played much football. He didn't play at all in high school. In all the years he's been out of football, I don't think he's gone to a game. Besides football, I also don't think he's ever really worked a day in his life—but then I haven't either.

Not working never bothered Ben or me. But it bothered George Buehler that he wasn't a doctor like his father, like his uncle, like his brother. He wasn't even a medical technologist like his sister. Every so often, especially in training camp, this 6'2", 260-pound guard from Stanford got depressed because he had gone into football instead of medicine. He would talk to me as if he had betrayed his family heritage.

"Don't worry about it, George," I always told him. "I'm sure your family is as proud of you as you are of them."

Maybe his complex about not being a doctor was why George sometimes seemed to be up on his own cloud. During the warmup once in San Diego, he tapped me on the shoulder and pointed toward the Chargers where a big white-haired man was walking around. "Isn't that Tommy Prothro?" he said.

"Yeah, that's him."

"What's he doing here?" George said.

"He's the coach."

"I thought he's the UCLA coach," George said.

"He's here now," I said.

My starting right guard didn't know the Chargers had hired Tommy as their coach. Another time we were in Pittsburgh, trying to hold onto a lead in the final minutes. In the huddle, George suddenly stared at Gene Upshaw's shoes.

"Your shoes are different from mine," George said. "Are they good on this surface?"

Once, we were getting ready to play the Chargers, which meant George had to block Louie Kelcher, their 300-pound defensive tackle, if our offense was going to do much. In our meeting that week, I emphasized how important it was to control Kelcher if we were to win.

"Number seventy-four," I kept saying. "We've got to block number seventy-four if we're going to win."

After the meeting Gene Upshaw tore some white adhesive tape into strips and formed a "74" on our big, red Coke machine—which wasn't much bigger than Louie Kelcher himself.

"George," he said, "if you can block the Coke machine, you can block Kelcher."

George put on his helmet and started slamming into the Coke machine. At the Coliseum the day of the game Gene taped a "74" on the Coke machine outside our locker room.

"George," he said, "you better warm up on the Coke machine."

You can laugh if you want, but George had his best game against Kelcher that day. George wasn't dumb. Nobody out of Stanford is dumb. But he was different. One year at training camp his room at the El Rancho was across a small courtyard from the room that served as a Raider office. One by one, the players would stop by the office for their mail. To save a few steps, George worked for weeks on a little remote-control car with a clamp on it. The idea was for the car to go across the courtyard to the office, where somebody would put his mail in the clamp, then the car would return by remote-control to his room. Day after day, the car would work okay until it tried to cross the grass in the courtyard. Finally, in the last few days of training camp, it worked.

"Modern technology," George shouted in triumph. "Modern technology!"

Training camp always gave players time to think. Dave Dalby, only the second center the Raiders ever had in their first two decades, used that time to be "commissioner" of all the spare-time tournaments the players had in bowling, shuffleboard, darts, bumper pool.

But others used that time differently. Harry Schuh used it to eat when he was supposed to be dieting. Harry was an All-AFL offensive tackle, 6'3" and listed at 260, but he was 280—and that reluctantly. Before he went to bed he would finish off a whole pizza by himself, then wash it down with a Diet Pepsi to show he was trying to lose weight. When nobody was looking, he would eat candy bars that he hid under his bed. After lights out, his roommate Wayne Hawkins pretended to be asleep until he heard Harry tearing the wrapper on a candy bar.

"Got ya!" Wayne yelled.

Sometimes a veteran who was afraid of losing his job would use the time at training camp to con a rookie. Ken Herock, a Raider tight end my first year as an assistant coach and now the Tampa Bay Bucs' player-personnel director, told me that his rookie year, another tight end gave him some advice.

"To keep your weight up in these two-a-day practices," the other tight end said knowingly, "you've got to drink beer in between."

Every day after lunch, the other tight end took Ken over to a nearby bar. For more than an hour before the afternoon meeting he would keep buying Ken beers while sipping one or two himself.

"By the time I got back," Ken once told me, "I had a headache. I couldn't remember the plays."

He remembered enough to make the team. At training camp a few years later, Ken decided to bust out one night before bed-check. He took the old standup lamp in his room at the El Rancho and stuffed it under the blankets on his bed, with the shade near the pillow. At a quick glance, it looked as if a body was under the blankets. Ken took off. Pretty soon Charlie Sumner, one of the assistant coaches, came by, checking each room. Charlie opened the door to Ken's room and flipped the light switch.

The lamp lit up under the blankets. Ken had forgotten to unplug it!

Skip Thomas once used some of his time at training camp to pretend he was Evel Knievel in a Raider helmet. Alonzo (Skip) Thomas was a cornerback out of SC who had a motorcycle. On a Saturday afternoon before a pre-season game in Oakland, we were sitting around our rooms waiting to leave at four o'clock in our chartered buses. To kill some time, Skip turned on his TV set to a program where Evel Knievel was soaring over something on his motorcycle. About half an hour later, I heard a knock on my door.

"Coach," one of the equipment men told me, "you better come out here. Skip thinks he's Evel Knievel."

Out in back of the motel, Skip had put some boards

up against the top of the big fence to form a runway. Maybe twenty feet beyond the fence, he had piled hay to cushion his landing. By the time I got out there, Skip had his Raider helmet on and he was revving his motorcycle.

"What the hell is this?" I yelled.

"I'm just having some fun, coach," he said. "I'll be all right, it's safe."

"The hell it is. Get off that bike."

He got off, then I told him to put the motorcycle in Dave Dalby's van, which Dave was driving to the game.

"Get that bike home," I roared, "and leave it there."

Skip was known as "Doctor Death," a nickname Bob Brown gave him. Most people thought he got it because of the way he played, but it really was because of the way he looked, at least the way "The Boomer" thought he looked.

"You're so ugly," The Boomer once boomed, "you look like Doctor Death."

In time, Skip got to be known simply as The Doctor or Doc, which once confused Charles Philyaw, a big defensive end. Charles got confused occasionally, like the time he informed me that he wanted his full name on the back of his jersey. I told him that the NFL only permitted a player's last name, unless there were two players on the same team with the same last name. In that case, a first initial was used.

"But not both their first and last names," I said.

"No, no," he said. "We got a guy who has his first and last name on his jersey."

"Who?" I said.

"Van Eeghen."

His confusion with Skip developed on a road trip

when Charles went to the room of our trainer George Anderson to borrow our portable whirlpool machine.

"I don't have it," George said. "Doc's got it."

Charles checked the roomlist and went to the room Skip shared with Jack Tatum.

"I need the whirlpool," Charles said.

"I don't have the whirlpool," Skip said.

"The trainer told me you had it."

"The trainer's wrong," Skip said.

Charles went back to George Anderson's room and told him Doc didn't have the portable whirlpool.

"I gave it to him," George said.

"He's not using it," Charles said, "and Jack isn't using it either."

"Jack who?"

"Jack Tatum."

"What the hell is Jack doing in Doc's room?"

"Jack rooms with Doc."

"No, no, no," George said. "I told you I gave the portable whirlpool to the Doc, but I meant the real Doc— you know, Dr. Fink, the team doctor."

"Oh, that Doc," Charles said.

Skip had a way with words. On the Friday before every home game I always took two players with me to our Booster Club luncheon, the one Skip called a banquet.

"Coach," he kept saying, "when are you going to take me with you to the banquet?"

"All right," I finally said, "two weeks from Friday. Remember now, Skip, two weeks."

Remember—hell, he wouldn't let me forget. Every day for the next two weeks, he had a question for me about his "banquet" appearance.

"What do I have to wear to that banquet, coach?" he would say.

"Just look nice," I told him. "That's all you have to do, Skip, just look nice."

"Do I have to speak at that banquet, coach?"

"Yes, you have to speak—you have to answer questions."

"I'm not speaking."

"You have to speak," I told him.

"All right, I'll speak."

Skip roomed with Jack Tatum for scholarly reasons. In those years, Skip and Willie Brown were our cornerbacks, Jack and George Atkinson were our safeties. Skip was from Southern Cal, Willie from Grambling, Jack from Ohio State and George from Morris Brown, which he called "the Harvard of the South"—but Skip had an answer for that.

"Morris Brown isn't a *university*," Skip would say, "and Grambling isn't a *university* either. Jack and me got to hold the defensive backfield together because we are the only ones from *universities*."

Marv Hubbard also was from a university, Colgate, a small school in upstate New York, but as our eleventh-round choice in 1968, he was cut. We liked him. We just got caught in a roster squeeze. We hoped nobody would pick him up, but the Broncos did, then they cut him too. He went to Hartford in the Atlantic Coast Football League, which he led in rushing with 899 yards. We brought him back to our 1969 camp, my first as a head coach. I knew he was going to make the team this time, but he didn't know it. The day we had to cut to fifty players, he wasn't at practice.

"Check his room," I told one of the equipment boys. "Maybe he got sick."

He wasn't sick. He was in his room, playing his guitar. The equipment boy talked him into coming over to practice. I was waiting for him in the locker room.

"Where the hell have you been?" I said.

"A year ago to the day, that's when I got cut," he said. "But nobody told me until a day later. I practiced an extra day. I didn't want to practice an extra day this year after I got cut."

"You're not cut," I said.

"I can read the handwriting on the wall," he said. "I know I'm cut."

"You're going to make the team."

"I am?" he said, still not sure.

"I'm telling you," I said, "you're going to make the team."

"Hey, let's go!" he said.

Marv had an angelic face, boyishly handsome. He wore white shoes and he was from Colgate, which some people think is an Ivy League school, maybe because it sounds like it should be. But he was one of the toughest, fightingest guys I've ever known, 6'1" and 215, from Salamanca, New York, a little town not far from Buffalo down near the Pennsylvania border. At training camp one year he got into a brawl in a bar. The next thing he knew, he was being sued.

"Where I come from," he said, "you go in a bar, you get in a fight, you prop the guy up, buy him a beer, you put your arm around him and you're buddies. And if you break something, you pay the bartender. Out here, if you get in a fight, some silly bastard sues you."

Once he took that "if you break something, you pay..." a little too far. After a game in Oakland, some of the players liked to gather at Clancy's bar in Jack London Square, a big Raider hangout. Everybody had a good time, especially when the Raiders won, but Marv's night wasn't complete until he broke the dry-cleaner's window next door. Marv was proud of being able to break glass without even scratching himself. He knew how to punch it and pull his hand back before the glass cut him. Whenever he left Clancy's on a Sunday night after we won, he would hand the bartender fifty dollars.

"That," he would announce, "is for the window next door."

We weren't losing many games in those years, especially at home. Which meant the lady who owned the dry-cleaners lost a lot of windows. After a few weeks, I got a message to phone her. She told me how she didn't want to call the police but that if it happened again, she would. I called Marv in and asked him if it were true.

"Yeah, it's true," he said, "but I always leave her fifty dollars."

"That's not the point," I said. "When the window's broken like that, people could walk in and steal clothes during the night."

"No problem, I won't do it anymore."

Marv had a different sense of honor. He and Bob Zeman, our defensive backfield coach, once were playing liars' dice with dollar bills.

"I call you," Bob said.

"Nine 6's," Marv said. "I got nine 6's."

"Let's see them."

"No, no, I don't have to show them. You have to believe me. In this game, you have to trust the other guy."

"I trust you, but let's see them."

"Are you accusing me of cheating?"

"No, but you got to show them to me."

"The hell I do," Marv said. "I won."

When we had a little field-goal kicker named George Jakowenko, he roomed with Marv awhile in training camp. Jak went to Syracuse, which isn't far from Colgate; that was reason enough to think they might have something in common. But the first week, Marv walked into my office.

"I want another roommate," he said.

"What's wrong with Jakowenko?"

"He wears pajamas," Marv said.

"What's so terrible about that?"

"I don't room with anybody who wears pajamas."

"You'll get used to them," I said.

The way I got the story later, Jak liked to write letters to his wife and go to sleep early, which wasn't exactly Marv's style. Eventually Jak's wife called me.

"I don't want my husband rooming with Marv Hubbard," she said. "He's a bad influence."

Marv was a bad influence on opposing linebackers too. He once told the writers about sticking his shoulder into Willie Lanier of the Chiefs, one of the best linebackers in the NFL, and hearing "all the air go out" of Willie's belly. The next time we played the Chiefs, he had a new nickname—"Old Mother Hubbard." But our linebackers loved him.

One night in 1976 at training camp, I was told that Ted Hendricks had not been in his room for bed-check. That was a five-hundred-dollar fine. The next morning I called him into my office.

"Where were you last night?" I said.

Some guys would make up a story about their aunt being ill, or their dog getting hit by a car, but not ol' Kick-'em.

"I went out with Hubbard," he said.

"What do you mean, out with Hubbard?"

"Well, he got cut yesterday. It was his last night here before he went home, it was his last night as a pro. I just decided to go out with him and celebrate."

I thought a moment. "I would've done the same thing. No fine."

8

Quarterbacks

YOU'VE PROBABLY HEARD THAT OLD SAYING—when the going gets tough, the tough get going. Kenny Stabler was like that, only better. When the going got hot, he got cool. The hotter it got, the cooler he got. Which made for a good mesh with me. The hotter it got, the hotter I got. Everything he was, I wasn't. Especially that 1977 afternoon in Baltimore, during an AFC divisional playoff game that went into overtime at 31–31. Not regular-season overtime where, if nobody scores after fifteen minutes, the game is declared a tie. This was playoff overtime where the game's not over until somebody scores, even if it takes until midnight. And through the first fifteen minutes of overtime, nobody scored. But we had begun to move the ball. With a first down at the Colts' thirteen-yard line, Kenny walked over to me at the Raider sideline during the automatic time-out before the second overtime period.

"All right," I said, "now let's..."

I was waving my arms and suggesting two or three plays that I thought might work. But then I realized that Kenny didn't seem to be paying attention. Behind his scruffy beard, he was gulping water from a paper cup and staring up into the stands at Memorial Stadium where many of the 60,730 people were on their feet.

"You know what, John?" he said.

"What, what?" I said. "Know what?"

"All these people," he said, looking around at the crowd, "are really getting their money's worth today."

"Yeah, yeah, they sure are," I ranted, then went back to talking about the plays. When he went back on the field, he hit Dave Casper in the end zone for the touchdown that won, 37–31, one of the greatest games I was ever involved in. It had everything—scoring, defense, passing, running, drama, overtime. As great as it was, we never had time to enjoy it. As soon as it was over, we sat in our locker room and watched the Broncos–Steelers playoff game until it was time to get on the buses to the airport.

It wasn't until then that I realized here was my quarterback in sudden-death overtime and he's thinking about the fans getting their money's worth.

In a game like that, sometimes you think you're in the middle of World War III or doing brain surgery. But with that one line, Kenny put it all in perspective. He also put himself in perspective. If the Raiders had a big lead, he usually got bored and sloppy. But if the Raiders were behind, he would get that look in his eye. The season after I stopped coaching, I was sitting with some friends watching TV—the Raiders in New Orleans in a Monday night game. The Saints jumped to a 28–7 lead in the second quarter, but then they made a mistake. They knocked Kenny on his ass. Suddenly a quick shot of Kenny's face appeared on the screen.

"Oh, oh," I said, "this game's over right now."

"It sure is," one of my friends said. "The Raiders are down by three touchdowns."

"No, no," I said, "the Raiders are going to win."

"What are you talking about?" somebody else said.

"That look in Kenny's eye," I said. "I've seen that look before. You wait. He'll win this game for the Raiders in the second half. You wait and see."

In the fourth quarter, Kenny threw three touchdown passes and the Raiders won, 42–35.

That's what made Kenny Stabler one of the best quarterbacks ever to play the game. I'm not going to rate quarterbacks here other than to say that Kenny was the best I ever had, and that Joe Namath and Terry Bradshaw, in that order, were the best I ever coached against. Quarterback is a lonely position. When his team wins, a quarterback gets too much credit. When his team loses, a quarterback gets too much abuse. It's tough for a quarterback to keep his perspective. But the great ones do.

Joe Namath was a great one. On his bad knees, he couldn't scramble. He should've been a sitting duck for pass-rushers. But they seldom got to him.

If he had good pass-protection, Joe threw the eyes out of the football. If he didn't have good pass-protection, he still got rid of the ball before he got sacked. The few times he got sacked, he was never intimidated. He projected an image of the quarterback in the white shoes who lived in a bachelor's pad with a white llama rug. Not exactly macho. But he was one of the toughest football players I've ever seen. In a Monday night game in 1972 at Oakland when we held on to win, 24–16, he threw for 403 yards, completing 25 of 46 passes against defenses stacked against him. I never did this before or since as a coach, but after that game I went over to the Jets' locker room.

"I just want you to know that I think you're great," I told Joe. "We had five or six defensive backs in there sometimes and you *still* picked us apart."

Terry Bradshaw was great in a different way. He was bigger and stronger than most quarterbacks. If he got trapped, he didn't scramble. He took off and ran like a fullback. With most quarterbacks, if a defensive lineman gets a hand on them, they go down like a bowling pin. But not Terry—he had to be tackled. He had another great quality. Most quarterbacks either have a good game or a bad game. But Terry could be off for three quarters and then throw three touchdown passes in the fourth quarter. Kenny Stabler was a fourth-quarter passer too. The tougher the game at the end, the tougher he was. In the fourth quarter, the best quarterbacks usually find a way to win. My last season as coach, Kenny found a new way. We were in San Diego, losing 20–14, our ball at the Chargers' 14-yard line with 10 seconds left. During our last time-out, we decided on which pass plays to use.

"No more time-outs," I reminded him as he turned to go back to the huddle. "You can't take a sack. You've got to get rid of the ball. If you're sacked, the game's over."

At the snap, Kenny went back to pass but none of his receivers were open. Woodie Lowe, a Charger linebacker, grabbed him by the jersey and spun him. As Kenny was falling, he fumbled the ball forward toward

Pete Banaszak near the 10-yard line. When Pete realized he was about to be tackled, he swatted the ball forward toward Dave Casper, who dribbled it from the 3-yard line into the end zone and fell on it. Touchdown, with no time left on the clock. When the Chargers started screaming that what Kenny did should have been ruled intentional grounding, I ran out on the field into the crowd around the officials.

"What are you doing here?" one of the officials yelled.

"Oh, I thought we had an injured player," I told him.

The touchdown stood, and then Errol Mann kicked the extra point. We won, 21–20, thanks to three football players who created what is remembered in San Diego as the "immaculate deception." That's finding a way to win. Not that Kenny had to be taught that, but his Alabama coach, Paul (Bear) Bryant, always talked about having to "play hard in the fo'th quarta." I think that impressed Kenny, just as it apparently impressed Joe Namath, another of Bear's boys. Bear once told me, "Stabler's better than Namath," but he loved them both.

I don't know if Bear knew how to coach it better than anybody else, but those two Alabama quarterbacks each had the one thing every great passer has— a quick release. To me, there's a mental mechanism that goes from a quarterback's eyes to his brain to his arm. The great quarterbacks never stop and think about throwing a pass. From the time they see a receiver getting open until the time the ball leaves their hand— zip, that's a quick release. Some quarterbacks seem to be saying to themselves, "I see the receiver... I cock my arm... I throw." By the time they do that, the receiver is usually covered.

But it takes more than just a quick release. Back in the years when Kenny was our third-string quarterback—behind Daryle Lamonica and George Blanda—his best friend and roommate was Tony Cline, a defensive end from Miami (Florida) University who had to lift weights to keep himself at 245 pounds. After we put Tony on a weight program, he pumped iron with Tom Keating, Fred Biletnikoff, and a few others every morning. At first, Kenny rode over with Tony from their apartment and disappeared into the trainer's room to read the newspapers.

"If you're going to be here with us," Tony finally told him, "you've got to do what we do."

Kenny soon was bench-pressing three hundred pounds. His chest got bigger. His shoulders got bigger. His arms got bigger. And in practice, he was throwing the ball better. That's when I realized that not only is it a good idea for a quarterback to lift weights, but he *must* lift weights. Not only for their arms, but also for their own protection. When they get hit, the upper body can absorb the blow better.

But as dependable as Kenny was during the season, that's how undependable he was during the off-season. As soon as our last game was over, he was a different guy. He reminded me of kids I knew when I was growing up. During the school year, they got good marks and did their homework. But when summer vacation started, they liked to raise a little hell. The years Kenny was with the Raiders, he was like that. As soon as his "vacation" started, he was back in Gulf Shores, Alabama, driving his pick-up truck, fishing, drinking. My first few years as head coach, whenever I brought in all our quarterbacks during the off-season for three days of meetings, I always had trouble finding him.

But the more I thought about it, the more I realized the off-season was his time, not mine. At training camp that year, I mentioned it to him.

"I'll make a deal with you," I said. "I won't mess with your time in the off-season and you don't mess with my time from training camp through to the end of the season."

"You got a deal," he agreed.

The only time I ever saw Kenny in Oakland during an off-season was the time he came to Oakland with his attorney, Henry Pitts, to negotiate a new contract. (It's funny how a player will always find time for that.) Anyway, they negotiated most of the contract with Al Davis, but then Al had to leave for an NFL owners' meeting.

"We're pretty close," Al told me. "You can finish it up."

I met with Kenny and Henry in Al's office after most of the staff had gone home. As I remember, we had to talk about a loan. But knowing Kenny, if they didn't like the deal, he might jump up and go home without signing. I sure didn't want that to happen. I had an idea. In order to make sure they stayed there until the deal was signed, I told the only other person in our office, Ken Bishop, to lock the door after he left. That way, if Kenny and Henry tried to leave, they couldn't get out and I would pretend I didn't have a key. Perfect. Except that a few minutes after Ken Bishop left, Henry studied the contract and smiled.

"Looks good to me, Kenny," he said. "Go ahead and sign it."

Kenny signed it, then he stood up and we all shook hands. They didn't know that we were locked in the office and I didn't dare tell them. I kept talking for a few minutes, then I suggested that they look around at all the pictures in Al's office. I hurried into another office and phoned one of the staff who lived nearby and had a key. In about fifteen minutes, I heard the door open. We talked some more, then I stood up.

"Hey, contract negotiations are easy," I said. "Let's have dinner."

At that stage of his career, Kenny Stabler was our quarterback. But he paid his dues. Like just about every NFL coach at one time or another, I had coped with a two-quarterback situation early in the 1973 season with Daryle Lamonica and Kenny—actually a three-quarterback situation because George Blanda wanted to play, too. Some coaches consider that a problem, but I never did. If anything, I liked it. Anytime I had a backup at a position who thought he should be the starter, it didn't bother me how much he complained to the media or to the other players or even to me. To be good, a football player needs a competitive nature. Anybody with a competitive nature wants to play.

When a guy doesn't want to play, you're really in trouble, especially if he's a quarterback. I've known some quarterbacks who were perfectly content standing on the sideline with a telephone headset and a clipboard. Play—hell, they knew if they played, they'd blow their cover.

I remember when George Mira was the 49ers' backup to John Brodie at quarterback. George had the best job in football. Whenever Brodie had a bad game, the fans in San Francisco would start chanting, "We want Mira, we want Mira." When the fans didn't get him, Mira told the writers, "Play me or trade me."

When the 49ers finally played him, he had his problems.

I think some NFL teams mishandle a two-quarterback situation. Either they try not to talk about it, or they prolong deciding between them because they're afraid to hurt a quarterback's feelings, usually the older quarterback. But all they do by prolonging the decision is hurt somebody's feelings even more.

To me, communication between a coach and his players was being able to say good things, bad things, and average things. Conversely, it's being able to listen to good, bad, and average things. Both ways, communication is also being able to do it with the same attitude. Don't avoid unpleasant things. Just go on and tell the person who has to hear it.

Some teams think a two-quarterback situation is divisive, that the players will take sides. I disagree. Most players just worry about doing their own jobs within the framework of the team. If an offensive tackle, for example, is trying to block a defensive end, he's not thinking about who the quarterback is behind him. In any controversial situation on a team, I think the players are the last ones to care. The coaches, the media, the fans are all more involved in it. In my experience, the players usually joked about it.

Looking back, it's hard to believe that going into the 1973 season Kenny Stabler had started only two games in the five seasons after the Raiders chose him in the second round of the 1968 draft.

His first year, he had a bad knee. His second year, he went home because of some family problems. So his third year was really his rookie year. But early in the 1971 season, he led us to a 27–16 win in Denver after Lamonica got hurt early in the first quarter. By the 1972 season, he started to come on strong. In our AFC playoff game at Pittsburgh that year, Daryle started, but Kenny's 30-yard scramble put us ahead, 7–6, before the Steelers won in the last few seconds when Franco Harris scored on his "immaculate reception." When we opened the 1973 season at Minnesota, my starter was Daryle, but he had some problems in a 24–16 loss. The next week Daryle started our home opener at Cal Stadium in Berkeley against the Super Bowl VII champions, the Miami Dolphins, who were on an eighteen-game winning streak that included their perfect 17–0 record the season before. We won, 12–7, on George Blanda's four field goals. The next week in Kansas City we lost, 16–3—two games without a touchdown. Near the end, I put Kenny in. The next day, Kenny walked into my office.

"I want to play, not just mop up," he told me. "Give me a chance to win or lose the game, not mop up."

"If you want to be the starter, fight for it," I told him. "Don't talk about wanting it. Make it happen."

On our defensive day that week, Kenny, as usual, took the part of the opposing team's quarterback. He also took the bull by the horns. Daryle hadn't done anything wrong. Kenny just seemed to want the job more. That's when I made up my mind that Kenny was my quarterback. I knew what I was going to do, but until I told Daryle face to face, I didn't want to risk being talked out of it. The next morning, I called Daryle into my office.

"I'm starting Kenny this week," I said. "I don't know how long he'll stay the starter. Maybe forever. Maybe it won't work out."

After the season ended, Daryle signed with the Southern California Sun of the World Football League.

But I had learned not to be wishy-washy about a two-quarterback situation. You can't have two starters. You can rotate three wide receivers or three running backs, but you can use only one quarterback. You can't appease the backup. You can't con him that he's going to play because he knows he's not. You have to say, this guy is it. You can change your mind later on and say, he's no longer it, the other guy is it now. But you've always got to have an *it*.

In his six seasons, Daryle had been something special. He had led us to five divisional titles. He threw 145 touchdown passes, 26 more than any other quarterback in that span. He had been the AFL's most valuable player twice, in 1967 and 1969.

Daryle had joined the Raiders at just the right time, in a 1967 trade with the Bills for quarterback Tom Flores (who later returned as one of my assistant coaches and eventually succeeded me) and wide receiver Art Powell, one of the AFL's best players in its early years. That's the season the Raiders really started to become the Raiders, not because I was a new assistant coach that year but because Al Davis had begun to make some important moves. When he returned to the Raiders in 1966 after being the AFL Commissioner for a few months, he suddenly was a part owner, the managing general partner. But for Al, that wasn't enough action. He started to concentrate on personnel—the draft, scouting, trades. In addition to his trade for Daryle in 1967, he signed George Blanda and he got cornerback Willie Brown from the Broncos in a trade—two Hall of Famers for virtually nothing. He also drafted Gene Upshaw, a future Hall of Famer.

Daryle Lamonica was the perfect quarterback for the Raiders at that time. He wasn't intruding on a team that was set. Instead, he eased into a team that was being built, a team that went to Super Bowl II that season, a team that was starting a tradition of success.

In those years, most teams used man-to-man defenses against the pass, not the zone defenses they went to later. With his strong arm, Daryle could throw against a man-to-man as well as anyone. Against a man-to-man, a quarterback usually can predetermine his receiver. Daryle loved to zoom in on one receiver, either Fred Biletnikoff short or Warren Wells deep. Daryle loved to throw deep. "The Mad Bomber," they called him. In his six seasons as the starter, he threw 32 touchdown passes from 40 or more yards away.

Some people thought Daryle threw too deep too often, especially at Baltimore in the 1970 AFC championship game we lost, 27–17, but I never complained. In those years against a man-to-man, I never thought you could throw too deep too often.

In a passing offense, the idea is to force the defense to cover as much of the field as possible in order to spread it out. If you throw deep, you really spread it out. If you throw short, you make the area that has to be covered smaller. If you've got a cornerback thinking that you're going to throw a 50-yard pass, he's concerned about covering your wide receiver over a 50-yard area. By throwing deep, you loosen up those cornerbacks and safeties. Even a long incomplete pass keeps a defense guessing. The next time your wide receiver takes off, a cornerback has to turn and run with him. That's when your wide receiver can cut to the sideline or over the middle.

Daryle acted more like a linebacker than a quarterback. Very emotional. In contrast, George Blanda acted like the old pro he was. On the sideline, he would calmly sit on his helmet like he was watching practice. When he had to perform, he was just as cool, especially in 1970, *his year*, when he was *only* forty-three years old.

In our sixth game that season we had a 7–0 lead over the Steelers at Oakland when Daryle's back got twisted. George went in, threw three touchdown passes and kicked a 27-yard field goal. We won, 31–14, but nobody thought much about it at the time. That's what George was expected to do, that's what we expected George to do, that's what George expected himself to do. Even at forty-three, even in his twenty-first season.

George had joined the Chicago Bears in 1949 when I was thirteen years old. After the 1958 season, the Bears released him, and in 1960 George went to the Houston Oilers for the AFL's first season when I was just starting at Hancock Junior College as an assistant coach.

But the difference in age was never a factor in our relationship. I can't ever remember George telling me that because he'd been around so much longer than I have, I ought to listen to him. The age thing never came up. I was the coach. He was the backup quarterback and the place-kicker. George didn't care how old I was any more than he cared how old he was.

His first season, George did what he was supposed to do. He led the Raiders in scoring, with 116 points on 20 field goals and 56 extra points. He didn't play much quarterback. He had been signed as a backup and he tolerated that role. But in practice, he began working with one of our new wide receivers, Warren Wells, throwing to him, talking to him.

His second season, we suddenly needed George to start a game in Denver when Daryle couldn't play. All week long, we had practiced a pass that isolated Warren Wells against a cornerback on a post pattern, meaning that Warren would run toward the goal posts. We just knew that this play was going to work when we needed it, and I assumed that George would save the play until he did need it. Or at least until he had good field position.

On the opening kickoff, a clipping penalty put us back on our own 6-yard line, first down. I figured George would use a couple of running plays from there. But on first down, whap, he threw to Warren Wells on that post pattern for 94 yards.

George was a grizzly, the toughest competitor I've ever seen. He had more pride in winning than anyone I've ever met. Anytime we didn't win, he figured that if he had been in there at quarterback, then we would have won. In the 1969 AFL championship game, one of the Chiefs' defensive ends, Aaron Brown, slammed into Daryle's passing hand. As he came to the sideline, Daryle was wringing his hand and wincing.

"You all right?" I asked.

"Yeah," he said. "Yeah."

He wasn't all right. His hand was badly bruised. But he wouldn't admit it to me or to our team doctor. That's all I had to go on—Daryle's word that he was all right. And in his mind, he was all right. X-rays the next day showed no fracture. Just because your quarterback is wringing his hand and wincing doesn't mean you take him out—especially a quarterback who has guided your team to a 36–4 record in regular-season games over three years. Later in that AFL title game, when I realized Daryle wasn't throwing properly, I put George in. He threw an interception but by then it didn't make any difference.

After we lost, 17–7, George was heard to complain that the game plan was "too long" and that I should have put him in earlier.

"I thought I could have moved the club," he said.

To hear some people, George should have been executed for treason. But his opinion didn't bother me. I would have been a lot more bothered if he *didn't* think he could have moved the club. As for the game plan being "too long," it's always too long. The game plan provides a quarterback with more plays than he needs. That's surely better than providing a quarterback with too few plays.

To me, the only important thing about George's complaint was that he wanted to win, and that he thought he would have been able to win. The next season, whenever Daryle got banged up—even if Daryle insisted he was all right—I didn't hesitate to put George in, like I did in 1970 in that 31–14 win over the Steelers, which turned out to be the start of something big.

The next week in Kansas City, only three seconds were on the clock when George's 48-yard field goal salvaged a 17–17 tie.

The next week, against the Browns in Oakland, we were losing, 17–13, when Daryle's left shoulder got banged up with 10 minutes left. With less than two minutes left, the score was still the same, fourth down and 16 at the Browns' 31-yard line.

"I hate to use the word," George admitted later, "but on that play I was scrambling."

On that play George found Fred Biletnikoff open at the 14 for a first down. Time out. At the sideline, I started giving him two running plays I wanted him to use.

"Go with the 16 Bob Trey O," I said, "then the 69 Boom."

In those situations, I always suggested plays to my quarterback. After all, I was the coach. But mostly, I believed in letting my quarterback call his own plays. He has a better feel for the situation on the field—his own players and the opposing players. If he knows he'll be calling his own plays, a quarterback will study films more, discuss the game plan with the coaches more. When the game starts, a quarterback must be a leader, a field general. How can he be a field general if he's waiting for instructions from the bench before every play? That limits his control, limits his leadership.

But during a time-out, I always talked to my quarterback about what plays to use, as I was that day against the Browns when I noticed George staring at me from behind the facebar on his helmet.

"What's the matter?" I asked.

"I'll do what you want me to do," George said, "but if you let me throw three slants to Warren Wells, I'll guarantee you a touchdown."

"You'll *guarantee* it?"

"I'll guarantee it."

"I can't guarantee the plays I gave you," I said. "Use the slants to Wells if you want to."

"You won't be sorry."

I wasn't. On first down, George looked for Warren, his favorite receiver, but he threw short. On second down, whap, he hit Warren for a 14-yard touchdown. George kicked the extra point and we were tied, 20–20, with a minute and 39 seconds left. In those years before overtime during the regular season, I was more than satisfied with a tie. Just keeping the Browns from winning was all I was thinking about until Kent McCloughan intercepted Bill Nelson's pass at midfield with 34 seconds left. But we didn't go anywhere. We had third-and-25 at our own 46 with no time-outs left when George threw a pass to Hewritt Dixon, who got out of bounds at the Browns' 45 with seven seconds left. We had no choice now but for George to try a 52-yard field goal.

"I think I put a little more rear-end into it than usual," George said later. "To give it more distance."

It sailed through with three seconds remaining. While we were covering the kickoff to preserve our 23–20 win, George walked over to me at the sideline.

"You know, John," he informed me, "this wasn't my longest. I had a 55-yarder once in Houston."

The next Sunday, in Denver, we were losing, 19–17, with about three minutes left. Daryle had thrown two touchdown passes but his left shoulder was still bothering him. I had thought about putting in George earlier but I didn't. In changing quarterbacks, a coach has to do it when the combination of the score and the time still makes it possible for the new quarterback to pull out the game. If it's a tie score, you can wait longer. If you're down by three points, you can't wait as long. If you're down by a touchdown or more, you can't wait at all. But being only two points down, all we needed was a field goal to go ahead. Daryle's shoulder was preventing him from pivoting properly and I just had a hunch that after what George had done the three previous games, he might give us a lift.

The first two plays, he didn't. But with a third-and-12 at our own 18-yard line, George hit Rod Sherman for a first down at our 45, then hit Warren Wells at the

Broncos' 20, then hit Fred Biletnikoff for a touchdown with 2:28 left. We won, 24–19.

When we got back to the Oakland Airport that night, about one thousand people were waiting for us. One big banner had "Blanda For President," another had "George Did It Again." The following Sunday, he did it one more time. There were about four-and-a-half minutes left, we were tied, 17–17, with the Chargers in Oakland, our ball at our own 27-yard line. But this time I kept Daryle in there. He moved us to the Chargers' 28, mostly on the ground. On a third-and-4 at the Chargers' 41, all his receivers were covered so he scrambled to their 28 for a first down. In three running plays, Charlie Smith got us to the 9 with 47 seconds left. As we let the clock run down, George was standing next to me. Time out with 7 seconds left.

"Go kick it," I said.

George had missed earlier from the 42 and 41 yards. But with the game on the line, I knew he wouldn't miss again. He didn't. We won, 20–17, on his 16-yarder with 4 seconds left. In the locker room later, Daryle pinned a "Blanda For Mayor" button onto his sweater. George had my vote, too. But his scenario had to end sometime. We went to Detroit for a Thanksgiving Day game with only three days' practice and a long plane ride. Not even George could save us from a 28–14 loss. For five weeks, though, he had been a hero to every middle-aged man in America—maybe every middle-aged woman, too. I knew he was a hero to his thirty-four-year-old coach, but he had been ever since I got to know him after Al Davis signed him as a free agent when the Oilers released him.

As much as George always wanted to play, and was always ready to play, he understood our quarterback situation. For five years, we had the ideal three types of quarterbacks. Daryle was in his prime as our starter. George was our backup who had the experience to take over in any situation. Kenny was our young quarterback, the one we were grooming, the one George was grooming, too. On the sideline, George would talk with Kenny about what was happening out on the field, and why. At their adjoining lockers during the week, George would talk to Kenny about being patient, about waiting for his opportunity.

"You're lucky you're here. This is a good team, a good organization," I heard George tell him once. "With a bad team or a bad organization, you might get beat up and never play."

As the coach, I told Kenny that too, but from George, it meant more. If a young quarterback isn't playing, he can go one of two ways—quit (which Kenny had done in 1969) or fight back (which George taught him to do). Kenny listened to George, like everybody else did. George could be ornery. He could cuss guys out for almost anything. For having a dirty locker. For belching. But not many players ever talked back to him. Daryle tried it once.

"George," he said, trying to be funny, "you made your reputation in the early years of the AFL throwing against weak defenses."

"I remember you at Buffalo throwing against the same defenses," George said. "You completed thirty-seven percent of your passes."

George and Kenny, of course, had a common bond. Each had been a college quarterback for Bear Bryant, though nearly twenty years apart—George at Kentucky in the 40's and Kenny at Alabama in the 60's. In the years when Kenny was hardly playing for us,

George asked me if Kenny could be his ball-holder for field goals and extra-points.

"It'll get him into the game," George said. "And the kid is a helluva holder."

"You're the kicker," I said. "If you want him as your holder, he's your holder."

Daryle had been George's holder, but I thought a starting quarterback should never be a holder, especially for field goals. Bad psychology. If we were kicking a field goal, it meant that our third-down play, probably a pass, had been unsuccessful in getting a first down. Which meant the quarterback was probably a little down. But as the holder, he had to be up, he had to be encouraging the kicker. That wasn't always easy. With a chance to be a holder instead of just standing on the sideline, I thought Kenny would be likely to be encouraging. And as George predicted, he was a helluva holder.

One of the toughest things I've ever had to do was cut George Blanda during our 1976 training camp. He was about to turn forty-nine years old. After twenty-six seasons, his leg just wasn't strong enough anymore. He had kicked 335 field goals, an NFL record. He had scored 2,002 points, an NFL record. And as a quarterback, he had passed for 26,920 yards and 236 touchdowns.

The weekend of his Pro Football Hall of Fame induction in 1981 at Canton, Ohio, the Blanda family drove over from Youngwood, Pennsylvania, where George had grown up. Saturday night he invited me to a party he had arranged for his family and his friends at a meeting room in a motel where they were staying. His eighty-five-year-old mother, Mary, was there along with his nine brothers and sisters with all their kids.

His brothers were just like George, big brawny guys. His brother Paul told me, "I don't know why everybody's fussing over the records George set. I've had five fathers-in-law." But when it got to be about one in the morning, the mother decided it was time for her to go to sleep.

"C'mon, Mom," one of George's brothers said, "I'll walk you to your room."

His mother glared at him. "Walk me to my room!" she said, wagging a finger. "You never walked me anywhere in sixty years, you're not going to start tonight. I'll walk to my room by myself."

Off she went. By herself. I know where George got it from.

9

Other Leaders

FROM THE SIDELINE, ALL I COULD SEE WAS Kenny Stabler down on his back like he was dead. In a 1977 game in Cleveland, one of the Browns' pass-rushers, Joe (Turkey) Jones, had hit him late. The only time a coach is allowed on the field is when one of his players is hurt, so I hurried out there. I was vehement. I was yelling at Jones and Mike St. Clair, the Browns' other big defensive end. I was pointing at them, calling them all sorts of names, really snarling. One of the Browns' defensive linesmen started to walk toward me. I thought to myself, *oh, oh, here we go*, but I didn't care. I was mad enough to fight him right out there on the field. That's when Art Shell turned toward him.

"You just get back there," big Art said, "and listen to the man."

Like a giant puppy, he went back and listened to me yell some more, just like big Art had told him to do. When even an opposing player listens, that's a leader. But it helps if you're a big leader. Art's big. He's 6′5″ and when he was playing, he was listed at 275 pounds and later at 285, but he was probably over 300 most of the time. I don't know for sure because I never bothered to weigh him.

"It's not what you weigh," I always told my players. "It's how you play."

Art played great. Not just good, great. He was an All-Pro offensive tackle three times, a Pro Bowl selection eight times. For all his weight, he was agile and quick. And a leader. By the nature of his role, a quarterback has to be a leader. But every team needs other leaders. In my years with the Raiders, we had at least half a dozen. Art Shell was one of our most effective leaders, even though he was one of our quietest guys. He's now a Raider assistant coach.

Mark my words, Art will be a head coach in the NFL someday. He's one of those guys you just respect. He's bright. He understands the game. And he's always been interested in all phases of the game—pass-patterns, the running backs, defense. Some players never think about anything except their own job, but Art always thought about everybody else's job, too.

"I was thinking last night," he would say to me every so often before practice, "when they're in this defense, maybe we should..."

At left tackle, Art had the toughest assignment on the offensive line. Most teams put their tight end next to the right tackle, which means the left tackle doesn't have the tight end to help him block. For that reason, most defensive teams put their best pass-rusher at right end in a matchup with the offensive left tackle. In our Super Bowl XI against the Vikings, big Art had the best game any offensive tackle ever had. He lined up against Jim Marshall, a strong, quick, experienced pass-rusher who was still a good player, not over the hill like some people thought. But that day Marshall never made a tackle.

As quiet as big Art was, Gene Upshaw was always a little hyper. Always up, always happy. If you were down and you talked to him, you soon were up. The way Gene is, if he were a dog, his tail would always be wagging.

Being a leader came naturally to Gene, the Raider offensive captain for more than a decade. He joined the Raiders in 1967, the same year I did. He was our first-round choice out of Texas A. & I. where he had been a center, tackle, and tight end. In those years, most guards were shorter and lighter than they are now, mostly because the defensive tackles were shorter and lighter. When the Packers won the first two Super Bowl games, for instance, their guards were Jerry Kramer at 6'3", 246, and Fuzzy Thurston at 6'1", 247— big, but not huge.

Gene was huge, 6'5" and 255, when Al Davis drafted him for a specific purpose—to block Buck Buchanan of the Chiefs.

Ever since Buck had joined the Chiefs in 1963, he had spent more time on the Raiders' side of the line of scrimmage than some of our halfbacks. Buck was 6'7" and at least 275 before dinner, the first of the huge defensive tackles. That same 1967 season the Chiefs had acquired Ernie Ladd, who was 6'9" and maybe 310, as their other defensive tackle. But Buck was the one we had to control. The season before, the Chiefs had gone to Super Bowl I, so if the Raiders were to go to Super Bowl II, we had to beat the Chiefs in our division. And if we were to beat the Chiefs, we had to block Buck.

As a rookie, Gene blocked Buck well enough for us to beat the Chiefs twice and go to Super Bowl II before losing to the Packers.

By the time he earned two Super Bowl rings, Gene was one of the NFL's most respected players, on and off the field. During the fifty-seven-day strike in 1982, he was the president of the NFL Players Association. (He later succeeded Ed Garvey as executive director.) I always thought that strike could have been averted. If you examine the eventual collective-bargaining agreement, it's clear that the dispute could have been settled without a strike if both sides had started serious negotiations earlier. When the owners got their $1 billion four-year TV contract with the networks, both the owners and the players knew how much money had to be shared. That's when serious negotiations should have started. I never thought the owners had to put up a tough front by hiring Jack Donlan as their Management Council negotiator, unless it was just to counteract Garvey representing the players. If some owners and players had sat down without Donlan and Garvey, they would have come up with a better deal for everyone.

Back when Gene was the Raiders' player rep, I was always able to talk out a problem with him. When we had the short strikes during training camp in 1970 and 1974, I figured if the players walk, they walk. When they walk back in, we'll play. But during the 1974 strike, some teams' players were reporting to camp anyway.

"Let's make a deal, Gene," I said. "Give me Stabler, Biletnikoff and the guys coming off injuries from last season. You can keep all the others on the picket line. I won't complain about them if you don't complain about the guys who come in."

Gene agreed. He knew as well as I did that it's important for a quarterback to work on his timing with his best receiver. So while Stabler was throwing passes in practice, Gene and the other players were carrying their picket signs outside. I was happy, they were happy. I had my quarterback throwing every day, that's all I cared about.

But we had our moments. Gene always had an answer for everything. Like the time he got a holding penalty in a big game with the Steelers.

To me, the biggest drive-stopper in football is a holding penalty. Your team is moving, then, boom, fifteen yards for holding. Now you're second-and-25. Against the Steelers that day, Gene was having trouble with Ernie Holmes, the Steelers' tackle. And just as we started moving, boom, he got a holding penalty. I was mad as hell, and Gene knew it. When he came off the field, I chewed him out.

"I didn't hold him," Gene said. "Believe me, I didn't hold him."

Hearing that, I started yelling at the officials that Gene hadn't held. Pretty soon, I forgot about it, especially when we won the game. But the next day, as I watched the film, there it was, right out there for everybody to see. Gene had his arms wrapped around Ernie Holmes, a clear holding penalty. The next day, I showed the team the film without a word to Gene, knowing that he would see that he deserved the penalty. After the film, I called him into my office.

"I thought you told me you didn't hold him," I said. "Hell, you damn near raped him."

Gene just sat there quietly, staring at me, then he said, "You want Snake to get killed?" He didn't say sacked, or hit, or hurt. He said *killed*. "If I hadn't held him," he said, "Holmes would've killed him."

I didn't know what to say to that. When I didn't say anything, Gene stood up and left. Out in the locker room, I learned later, he started telling the other offensive linemen that I had said it was all right to hold rather than get Snake killed. When that got back to me, I called Gene into my office again.

"And make sure," I told him this time, "you set the other linemen straight on holding penalties."

Those films never lie. Most players sit in that darkened room and wait for their big moment—a good block, a good tackle, a good catch, a good run. I always sat there with the clicker that stops the film, runs it backwards, then runs it forward. With most players, as soon as they saw themselves make a good play, they would say, "Hey, coach, let me see that again." But if they messed up, they never say a word. Except for Jim Otto, the Raider center for the first fifteen seasons of the franchise. He was an AFL original, 6'2" and 255 out of Miami (Florida) University who was the All-AFL center in each its ten seasons. His last few years, he played on guts. Now he's paying for it. He's got two bad knees. When he was inducted into the Pro Football Hall of Fame, he could just about walk up there to make his speech. But watching film, he always was more interested in his mistakes than his good blocks. He sat in the front row and listened to every word, good or bad. Whenever he made a good play, he never asked to see it again. He *expected* to make a good play. But as soon as he saw himself miss a block, he spoke up.

"Keep running that back and forth," he would say. "I want to see what happened here."

He would have me run that play ten or twelve times until he was satisfied that he knew what happened—so it would never happen again. By doing that, Jim taught me how every player should watch game films. For what he did wrong, not for what he did right.

"You've got to watch for what you don't want to see," I told our young players. "You have to listen to what you don't want to hear."

In watching film, the idea is for the players to see the good plays so that they know what to do again the next time, to see the average plays so that they would try to improve the next time, to see the bad plays so that they would correct them the next time.

"When we look at the bad plays, it's nothing personal, we're not trying to embarrass you," I told my players. "You have to look at the bad plays with the same mind that you look at the good plays."

Jim Otto was definitely a leader, but by the 70's, he was too old to relate to our younger players. That's one reason a team needs several leaders—to have somebody to relate to the various players, by position or by age. Or sometimes by example. Fred Biletnikoff led by example. Over his fourteen seasons, he was one of the best wide receivers ever to play the game. His 589 receptions for 8,974 yards and 76 touchdowns are Hall of Fame stats. At 6'1" and 190, out of Florida State, he wasn't really strong enough or fast enough to put those stats together. He did it with hard work. The first couple of weeks at training camp, we always had two practices—one in the morning, one in the afternoon. Two-a-days, the players called them. But after our afternoon practice, Fred would get a quarterback to throw to him while he ran patterns for half an hour, then he ran a few laps. When we went to one practice, he would do his extra work early in the morning.

Fred was a perfectionist. If he dropped a pass in practice, he would start cussing at himself. And after practice, he would punish himself. He would get Stabler or Lamonica to throw that pass and he would catch it as many as one hundred times.

Fred taught me what "good hands" were. We have these mysterious phrases in football that nobody ever defines. We say a pass-receiver has "good hands," but what exactly does that mean? As a college coach, I had never heard an explanation for it. One day at practice I was marveling at how softly he caught the ball with the good hands he was famous for.

"Tell me something, Fred," I said. "Just exactly what are good hands?"

"Good hands," he said, "means both hands work together. If your right hand reaches out for the ball, your left hand reaches out on the same plane. They move together. Guys with bad hands, when they reach out for a ball, only one hand moves. The other hand stays where it is."

"You mean your hands always move together?"

"Most of the time," he said. "Not always."

Every so often in practice, Fred would make what everybody else thought was a good catch. But he would slam the ball down and start cussing. He was an All-Pro cusser.

"What's wrong with you?" somebody would say.

"My hands weren't together," he'd answer.

When stickum got to be popular, the joke was that if Fred ever really put his hands together, he would be unable to pry them apart. He used more stickum than anyone else. He smeared it all over his hands and wrists, even up his forearms. He once leaped for a pass and the ball actually stuck to one of his forearms. Every time he caught a pass in a game, the officials had to throw the ball out of play. It had to be cleaned with a special solvent. Our center was responsible for making sure all the stickum was off the ball before it was snapped. Otherwise the ball would stick to the quarterback when he tried to pass or hand off.

The day of a game, Fred was always the first player in our locker room, sipping coffee and smoking cigarettes and tossing a ball in the air. Just before we went out for the warmup, he always tossed something else. His cookies. The closer it got to the warmup, the quieter it got in the locker room. Fred always went out at ten minutes after the hour with the specialists. At about eight minutes after the hour, Fred would be in the bathroom, heaving. I didn't need a watch to know what time it was.

"All right," I'd say, on hearing Fred, "everybody up for the warmup."

The strange thing is, I don't know what Fred threw up. He never ate anything at the pre-game meal. But once the game started, he was another person. Cool, tough.

Our "91 comeback" was his pet play. He could run a comeback off an out, meaning he could come back toward the ball after running a square-out pattern to the sideline. Fred ran that pattern better than anybody. When a wide receiver makes the cut toward the sideline, it's supposed to be sharp, a ninety-degree turn. He's not supposed to angle upfield at all. If he does, it gives the cornerback an interception angle on the pass. By running that square out, or "an out," as most coaches call it, you have a chance to beat the corner-back; if you come back down the field a yard or two, you have even a better chance. Fred would always run that square-out and then come back. He drove cornerbacks crazy, especially when he pivoted and got by them after he caught the ball.

That pivot move came from a tip from Eldridge Dickey, one of our wide receivers who had been drafted as a quarterback out of Tennessee State in 1968's first round. During a game Fred was tackled as he caught a pass on his "91 comeback" play. On the sideline later, Eldridge walked over to him.

"You don't have to get tackled on that play," Eldridge said. "You can pivot and run, you can still make some yardage."

If any of the coaches had suggested that to Fred, he might have forgotten about it. But when Eldridge mentioned it, Fred accepted it. Soon he was practicing pivoting and running. He made it one of his best moves.

Just as Fred never wanted to drop a pass, even in practice, over on the other side of the field, Willie Brown never wanted to let a receiver catch a pass, even in practice. Willie joined the Raiders as our right cornerback in a trade with the Broncos the same year I came on, 1967, and he stopped playing the same time I stopped coaching, after the 1978 season. In all those years, not many receivers caught a pass on him. Not in games, not in practice. That's one reason he's in the Hall of Fame now.

Some cornerbacks believe in the "cushion" theory. They let a receiver catch the short passes that don't produce a first down. Willie's theory was that you never let a receiver catch even one pass if you could help it. None. Never.

Willie wanted to pitch a shutout every game. Sometimes he did. His first few years, the Jets had a wide receiver named George Sauer, Jr., who was too tricky for most other cornerbacks, especially with Namath throwing to him. But against us, Sauer hardly caught a ball. Willie owned him.

Willie had a great moment late in his career and late in Super Bowl XI, when he returned an interception 75 yards for the touchdown that put the Vikings to bed. He deserved that moment.

To me, his greatest play occurred in Houston late in the 1973 season. We were ahead, when one of the Oilers caught a pass on the other side of the field. Willie started chasing him anyway and hauled him down on the 2-yard line. On the next play, the Oilers fumbled, Phil Villapiano recovered on the goal-line and ran it back 52 yards. We wound up winning, 17–6, but if Willie hadn't hauled down that receiver, we might have lost. The thing about that play was, Willie was so far away from the ball, if he hadn't chased the receiver, I wouldn't have noticed. Neither would any of my assistant coaches. Willie didn't have to chase that receiver, but he did—and caught him. That's what I remember about Willie Brown, that's what made Willie a leader.

Clarence Davis was a leader, and not just for his rushing yardage. Clarence was probably the best blocking halfback I've ever known. I never was interested in the great runner who couldn't block. To me, the most important thing about any play was the blocking. If you don't block properly, the play can't possibly work.

Pass-block or run-block, Clarence leveled people. He wasn't that big at 5'10" and 195 but long before he was a tailback at Southern Cal he was a guard in high school. His early training was as a lineman. He not only knew how to block, he enjoyed it. He had some big games. He ran for 137 yards in Super Bowl XI. And he could catch the ball. Putting everything together, he was the perfect halfback. Not many people realized what a good blocker he was, but the Raiders knew. His blocking ability set a standard. Not long after Marcus Allen joined the Raiders as the 1981 Heisman Trophy winner, I worked one of their exhibition games for CBS.

"Wait 'til you see Marcus," Tom Flores told me. "He can block as well as Clarence did."

I remember Pete Banaszak as a leader for a different reason—for being an old-fashioned player, a running back out of Miami (Florida) who was born about thirty years too late. He should have played when they wore leather helmets. Some guys look good in their underwear, but when they put the pads on and it's first-and-10, they don't do anything. Pete was just the opposite. Standing around, he was a stiff. Throw him a ball, chances are you would hit him in the head with it. He just was not a good athlete. At 6' and 210, he wasn't that big—but he never got hurt. After a tough run, he would come back to the huddle looking out the earhole in his helmet. But he never got hurt. He played in 105 consecutive games, a remarkable streak for a running back. The tougher the yardage, the better he ran. In short-yardage and goal-line situations, he was the best runner I've ever seen.

In Super Bowl XI, we had a 10–0 lead with a first down on the Vikings' 1-yard line. On the sideline, I was planning what play we would use on second down. But we never had second down. Pete rammed it in there on first down. He later scored from the 2-yard line.

Pete always found the hole. He hardly ever fumbled. And if you needed somebody for special teams, he was always available. He was a *professional football player*, the kind you win with, the kind you love. My son Joe almost left home with him once. Pete and Tom Keating had stopped by our house when they were bachelor roommates. As they were about to leave, Pete looked at Joe who was maybe three years old.

"C'mon, Joe," he said, "why don't you come to live with Tom and me?"

Joe never hesitated, never even looked at Virginia or me. He got his coat, put it on, and was ready to walk out the door. I knew the feeling. At the start of training camp in Pete's early years, some of our coaches, including me, always wondered if he would make the team. But as the season opener approached, he was always there. At camp after Super Bowl XI, the coaches were sitting around with Al Davis one night, talking about the roster limit of forty-three players.

"Just pick forty-two players," Al said. "You know John is going to keep Pete no matter what."

That training camp followed the trial of a $2 million slander suit filed by George Atkinson, our strong safety, against Chuck Noll and the Steelers. In our 1976 opener, George had whacked Lynn Swann across the helmet from behind with a forearm, knocking him unconscious. Back in Pittsburgh the next day Chuck charged that a "criminal element" existed in the NFL, that players like George "should be kicked out" of the league. Pete Rozelle fined George $1,500 for what he did; the commissioner fined Chuck $1,000 for what he said. George then filed suit for $2 million in damages. After a ten-day trial in a federal court in San Francisco, the jury decided: no slander, no malice, no damages.

On the witness stand, I spoke about how what George did to Swann had been a reaction, not premeditation.

On the play, Swann, a wide receiver flanked to the right, had run down the right sideline, then cut toward the middle of our zone defense where George was waiting to cover him. As the play developed, Terry Bradshaw, the Steeler quarterback, had to scramble before throwing a pass to Franco Harris, who caught the ball about fifteen yards away from George. But as Swann had cut into George's area, George took a swing at him. To me, that was an instinctive reaction by a safety, not a premeditated cheap shot.

"There's a difference between how a cornerback covers a wide receiver and how a strong safety covers a wide receiver," I remember testifying. "With a cornerback, a forearm is more likely to be premeditated because he's always covering that wide receiver. With a strong safety, who usually covers a tight end, that wide receiver is suddenly in his area and he reacts."

I think what still bothers George is that he was accused of premeditation. He was a terrific player for the Raiders for ten seasons. But most people remember him now only for that incident and that trial. I remember him more as the smallest strong safety in the NFL for most of his career. He was 6 feet and 165, not really big enough to cover those tight ends. But he covered them. And with his speed, I never had to worry about the other team isolating him on a wide receiver who could really run. George could run. When he arrived in 1968 as a seventh-round choice out of Morris Brown in Atlanta, he ran a 4.5 for 40 yards. That's not considered real fast today when many teams time their players running on artificial turf and wearing shorts. But when George ran 4.5 on grass, he was wearing football shoes and some equipment. At the time, 4.5 was the fastest any player had ever been timed with our stopwatches.

Some of those small, fast guys prefer to run away from trouble, but George was absolutely fearless. With a strong safety, you worry when he has to come up and force a sweep that is being led by those big guards, but George took on those big guards.

In the locker room, George was the leader of our defensive backs. Most of their lockers were together in the back of the room. The ghetto, they called it. In the morning, one of them would stretch a piece of tape across the ghetto to keep everybody else out. If another player tried to go in there who didn't belong there, they would tape him up and dump him in a trash can. But they never went too far. George enjoyed good-natured fun, but he never let it get mean or ugly. He knew when to cool it.

Out on the field, George was the same way. Anytime I saw the defensive backs doing something I didn't like, or if I didn't think they were paying attention in meetings, I told George. That's what I remember about George, not the slander suit.

But now that I think about it, I remember another suit. One of our rookies once got slapped with a paternity suit that went back so many years we figured he had to have been about twelve years old when he allegedly fathered the child. Some years after the suit was settled, I was on a bus going to our hotel on an early season road trip. I was sitting near several rookies, so I decided to give them some fatherly advice.

"Now that you've made the team," I told them, "you've got to watch out for people trying to take advantage of you."

I warned them that strangers and even old friends would be coming out of the woodwork to weasel money from them.

"You really have to be careful, look what happened to him," I said, motioning to the veteran who had been hit with the paternity suit. "When he was a rookie, he got a paternity that was so ridiculous, he had to be twelve years old when he fathered the child. Ridiculous."

Across the aisle of the bus, their teammate looked up. "It wasn't ridiculous, coach," he said. "It was true."

10

Draft Day

EXCEPT FOR THE DAY OF A BIG GAME, THE BEST day in pro football is the day the NFL teams draft college players. But it's not as complex as all those computers make it sound. In my years with the Raiders, it was as simple as a blackboard and a manila folder. Up on a big blackboard we had all the players rated in order by position. The same ratings were pasted inside a manila folder handed out to all the coaches, a trick Al Davis learned from Paul Brown back in the 50's. As a Colts' scout in those years, Al attended an NFL draft meeting where most of the personnel directors had big notebooks. But all Paul Brown had was a manila folder with his lists of players rated in order by position—running backs, linebackers, whatever. Just strips of names pasted inside the manila folder.

As the draft evolved every year, I always found it easier to check my manila folder than a computer. But one of the Raiders' best draft choices was never listed in our manila folders.

When the twelfth and last round of the 1977 draft began, we weren't that impressed with any of the names in our manila folders who were still available. None of us were willing to recommend any of those names—not Al, not me, not any of our assistant coaches, not any of our scouts.

"None of these guys is worth it," somebody said.

"You're right," I said. "Down at Southern Cal they have better players walking around the campus than any of the guys we're talking about."

"Who?"

"I don't know who," I said, "but I'll find out."

I phoned my buddy John Robinson, who had taken over as Southern Cal's head coach the previous season. I asked him if any of his players who hadn't been drafted yet had a chance to play in the NFL.

"Has Rod Martin been taken yet?" he said.

"Not the last time I looked," I told him.

"Rod's a better football player than anybody who's been drafted in the last five rounds," he said. "He'll make your team."

"That's good enough for me," I said. "Thanks."

I went back into our draft room and looked around at all our coaches and scouts.

"I got a name," I said. "Rod Martin, linebacker."

Half an hour later, we drafted him. We liked him in training camp, but we had to cut him and the 49ers claimed him. When the 49ers released him later on during the season, we signed him again. He's now an All-Pro linebacker, the Raiders' defensive captain on their Super Bowl XVIII team. I wasn't always that smart. Or that lucky. Like any other coach, I drafted my share of guys who couldn't play. That's the beauty of the draft. You never know when you're going to discover a diamond in the rough.

When the other NFL teams joined scouting combines, the Raiders declined. Al Davis didn't want to share information. He always felt our coaches and our scouts were looking for certain things in a player. When we found those things, we didn't want to have to tell other teams about those things.

Of all the draft choices the Raiders made in my time, the easiest was Ray Guy, the punter from Southern Mississippi who was also the most surprising choice. The moment we took him as the twenty-third player in 1973's first round, our phones started ringing. Everybody in the NFL was wondering why the Raiders would waste a number one choice on a punter. But in our offices that day, of all the first-round choices I have been involved in, Ray Guy was the only one our coaches and scouts agreed on unanimously.

Usually the offensive coaches want an offensive player and the defensive coaches want a defensive player. Usually a punter isn't even considered until the fourth or fifth round. But that year our offensive coaches wanted Ray Guy, our defensive coaches wanted Ray Guy, and the head coach really wanted Ray Guy.

During the previous season Jerry DePoyster had turned punting into an adventure for us. The last thing a coach wants to worry about is having a punt blocked. That year Jerry led the league with three blocked punts, which meant I led the league in worrying about it. Jerry's problem was that he didn't have sure hands. You want a punter who will catch the ball cleanly with his hands extended, turn it, and kick it. But he didn't trust his hands. He sort of caught the ball against his chest, which meant it took a fraction of a second for him to get the ball situated in his hands and to bring it out where he could kick it. That fraction of a second was all the other team needed to block the punt, or come close to blocking it. Instead of a punt being automatic, it became a play I dreaded. It's bad enough to punt from deep in your own territory without having to worry about the punt being blocked.

As a result, we were searching for a punter in 1973 when the best punter I've ever known was available. As soon as I saw a highlight film of Ray Guy punting for Southern Mississippi, I knew we had to take him in the first round. We had a good offense and a good defense. What we needed most was a punter who would get us the best possible field position. In scouting him on film, I remember him booting the ball 100 yards once, *more* than 100 yards actually. From his own end zone, he boomed the ball so far it landed at the other 20-yard line, more than 80 yards in the air, and bounced into the other end zone. I kept running that film back and forth to make sure I saw it right. The more I saw it, the more I knew we had to take him in the first round.

The day of the draft, we were sweating whether he would still be available when we picked. He wasn't a secret. He had led the nation with a 46.2-yard average, he had been a unanimous All-America selection. We had heard that another team, the Cowboys, was thinking about him. But when nobody else took him, boom, we sent his name right in.

Ray Guy was special. Tall with long legs, 6'3" and 190 pounds. One of those guys who comes along every ten years, if that. Most punters and place-kickers aren't really football players, but he had been an outstanding safety with 18 interceptions over three years. In high school he had been a quarterback and a big-league baseball prospect as a pitcher. He could throw a football further than any of our quarterbacks—eighty, ninety yards. Whenever Ray started to throw the ball after practice, our quarterbacks would disappear. He embarrassed them.

If a punter or a place-kicker is a real football player, he doesn't want to be known just as a specialist. George Blanda hated to be known as a kicker. He considered himself a quarterback who kicked. As a rookie Ray Guy considered himself a safety who punted. When he signed his contract, our people apparently told him that he would be looked at as a safety, but nobody ever told me. One of our first days in training camp, he ran out there on defense.

"No, no," I yelled at him, "you're our punter, Ray, we don't want you getting banged up."

"But they told me I'd get a shot at safety too," he said. "I'm not just a punter."

"After you get settled as a punter," I told him, "we'll take a look at you at safety."

I lied. I knew I'd never let him do anything but punt. Not after what I'd seen. He wanted to place-kick too, but if I had let him, he would not have been so great a punter. Place-kicking and punting use different muscles. When you place-kick, you shorten your foot and lengthen your Achilles tendon. When you punt, you lengthen your foot and shorten your Achilles tendon. I don't think anybody can do both well. His first day at training camp, he started punting for the writers and the photographers, who were inspecting him as our number one draft choice. Punt after punt, he was booming the ball about sixty yards in the air.

"That's good, Ray, that's enough," I said.

"I'm still warming up," he said. "I'm still stretching my leg. Let me get warmed up."

"Yeah, sure," I said. "Get warmed up."

Soon he was punting the ball seventy, eighty yards in the air. And he had good hands. He caught the snap cleanly, turned the ball and boomed it, his right leg following through above his shoulder. As a rookie with a 45.3-yard average, he was All-Pro for the first of six consecutive seasons. Over 10 years, he averaged 42.9 yards. I never remember him shanking a punt. One reason was that I never asked him to go for the coffin corner. Oldtime players and fans always ask me why most punters don't go for the coffin corner anymore, but I believe that leads to more shanked punts than to punts that go out of bounds inside the 10-yard line. I just wanted Ray to get it up high and try to bounce it inside the 5-yard line where the coverage could down it.

I was never much on hang-time until we got Ray, but then we started clocking how long his punt hung in the air. Sometimes he kept it up there as long as six seconds.

Ray loved to punt it high. In the warmup before the 1976 Pro Bowl at the Louisiana Superdome, he was punting balls so high, they were bouncing off the TV-screen gondola that hangs from the roof. That night the gondola was ninety feet above the field. In the third quarter, our AFC team was leading when he sidled up to me.

"Is it all right," he asked, "if I try to hit the gondola?"

"Hell, no, it's not all right," I barked. "This is a game."

He turned away, but then I started thinking that

the Pro Bowl is an all-star game, an exhibition, that he deserved the opportunity to put his punting prowess on exhibition.

"On second thought," I told him, "go for it."

The next time we had to punt, Ray boomed the ball up, up, up—whack, into the gondola. The crowd loved it. But the officials didn't. They knew how high Ray could punt. In the pre-game meeting, it had been decided that if any punt hit the gondola, the ball would be re-punted. Ray boomed it again, but took a little off it this time. Not much though. He averaged 47.4 on five punts that night. But all anybody talked about later was the one that hadn't counted in his average, the one that hit the gondola.

Another time, in a pre-season game in Detroit, I was ready to let Ray get tackled until I came to my senses. Just before the half, Ray punted, but we were penalized and had to punt again. Two seconds were on the clock. As our punting unit was about to huddle, I realized there was no need to punt. If we don't punt, the Lions can't get the ball and maybe return it for a touchdown.

"Ray, just run with the ball," I yelled.

But then I thought, Ray is too valuable for that. If he got tackled hard, he could get his golden leg hurt. Or even his other leg. Or any part of him.

"No, no, Ray, don't you run with it," I yelled, "let Van Eeghen run with it."

Our rookie fullback that year, Mark Van Eeghen, lined up as the blocker for Ray in punt formation. When the ball was snapped, the Lions turned to run back to block for their return. None of the Lions seemed to notice that the ball had been snapped to Van Eeghen, who started running with it as if he were chasing the

Lions instead of them chasing him. By the time the Lions realized we hadn't punted, he was on his way to a 63-yard touchdown.

"That was a great trick play," somebody said to me later.

"Yeah, well," I stammered, "that really surprised them."

At the time only two people thought that Mark Van Eeghen would turn out to be such a good fullback— Al Davis, who had spotted him working out in shorts and sneakers at a gym when the East–West practice was rained out, and Norm Van Brocklin, my pal from the Philadelphia Eagles who then was the Atlanta Falcons' coach. The day we took Mark in the third round of the 1974 draft, the Dutchman phoned me.

"What do you want for Van Eeghen?" he said.

"We just drafted him," I said. "We don't want to trade him."

"I'll give you anything you want."

"How come you're so high on him?"

"His name is Van Eeghen, he's Dutch," he said, laughing. "He's got to be great."

He was. In eight years, Mark developed into the Raiders' all-time leading rusher with 5,907 yards. He had three 1,000-yard seasons, with a high of 1,273 in 1977, the most yards a Raider back has ever had. And whenever Norm Van Brocklin saw me in those years, he would remind me of that conversation.

The draft always produces some strange phone calls from other teams' coaches and scouts. When we took Raymond Chester in the first round of the 1970 draft, we didn't know where we were going to play him. In his three seasons at Morgan State, he had been a tight end, a running back, and a linebacker. We needed a tight end. And we knew from the films that, at 6'3" and 220, he was big, strong, and fast. When we picked him, some clubs were shocked. In those years, not many small-college players were being taken in the first round. And some teams hardly scouted black colleges then. The day after that draft, Tom Fears, then the New Orleans Saints' coach, phoned me.

"John, be honest with me," he said, "is Raymond Chester really a player?"

"Hell, yes, he's really a player," I said. "We wouldn't have taken him in the first round if we didn't think he was a player."

"Have you seen him?"

"I've seen him on film. He can play. We're not sure of his position yet, but we're projecting him as a tight end. If not, he'll play somewhere."

"You think he's that good?"

"Absolutely," I told him.

"That does it," Tom said. "Nobody in our organization had him on their list as a draftable player or even as a free agent. You took him in the first round, but nobody here even thought he was good enough to put on their list."

I understand some people in the Saints' organization were fired over that.

Raymond Chester was a natural athlete who might have made it at running back or linebacker. We never bothered trying to find out. He just took over as our tight end. But for all our films and scouting reports, we didn't realize how tough he was until late in the 1972 season. We were getting ready to play the Chiefs in a big game. At practice Thanksgiving morning, Raymond was running his pattern on a pass play when he pulled a hamstring. It popped like a rifle shot and he toppled to the ground.

When he went to the hospital that day, I knew from experience that a pulled hamstring usually meant a player would be out six weeks.

But by Saturday morning Raymond was out of the hospital and standing around at practice. Sunday our team physician then, Dr. Graham Reedy, told me he thought Raymond could play.

"Are you sure?" I asked.

"His other muscles are so big and so strong," he said, "that the rest of the hamstring can carry the leg. I wouldn't use him unless you have to, but he can play if you need him."

When our other tight end, Bob Moore, got hurt, Raymond caught a touchdown pass that helped us win, 26–3.

Drafting players such as Ray Guy and Raymond Chester in the first round doesn't take much expertise. Those guys jump out of the films. To me, the trick in the draft is the players taken in the later rounds. In the fourth round in 1972, the Raiders had two choices. With the first we took Cliff Branch from Colorado, who turned out to be an All-Pro wide receiver. With the second, we took Dave Dalby from UCLA, who turned out to be Jim Otto's successor at center. Not that we knew they would be that good. At the time we considered each one to be a specialist—Cliff to return punts, Dave to snap on punts and place-kicks.

As a rookie, Dave was the best 15-yard snapper I've ever seen. He got the ball back there so quickly, I couldn't believe it. After a while, I realized that a center has to be young to snap that well. The longer they play, the more their shoulders, elbows, and hands get battered. Then they don't have the strength. Jim Otto had been a good snapper early in his career, but at the end, the ball floated the fifteen yards to the punters like the last shot out of a Roman candle. Snapping the ball to a punter is all arms and wrists, but it takes looseness. If a center has stiff arms and wrists, he can't do it nearly as well.

Right away, we knew Dave was the snapper we had been looking for; but with Cliff, we thought we had made a big mistake.

We knew Cliff wasn't just another world-class sprinter or hurdler who was hoping to play pro football. Most of those guys are track stars who are trying to play football. Cliff was like O.J. Simpson, Herschel Walker and Bob Hayes—a football player who also ran track. We had checked out Cliff's career. He not only had been an All-America wide receiver at Colorado but he had been an All-District wide receiver at Worthy High in Houston, where he grew up. He was the first Texas schoolboy sprinter to run the 100-yard dash in 9.3 seconds. As far as we were concerned, we had drafted a football player who could run, not a sprinter who might be able to play football. But when we put Cliff back there to return punts in training camp and exhibition games, he wanted to hurry toward the sidelines instead of darting upfield. In the NFL, they tackle too well for anybody to get away with that. When we used him at wide receiver, he didn't hold onto the ball. For all his speed, we figured we blew this choice. But one day during practice Fred Biletnikoff had a suggestion.

"Cliff's trouble," Fred said, "is that he's so fast and so hyper, when he runs, his eyes are bouncing. He never sees the ball coming into his hands. If he slowed down a little, he'd still be fast enough and maybe he'd catch the ball better. Let me work with him."

Fred soon had Cliff running under control. His eyes were no longer bouncing and he could make his cuts. Cliff was so fast, for him to be in control to make a cut at fifteen yards, he nearly had to come to a full stop, then make his cut. He was so fast that, if he ran full speed for five yards, it would take him the next ten yards to slow down enough to make a cut at fifteen yards. Fred taught him to cut off angles, not off straight lines. In college, Cliff had run in straight lines. He was so fast, he could get away with it in college. But in the NFL, you can't just be fast.

As a rookie, Cliff only caught three passes. Two years later, he caught 60 for 1,092 yards and 13 touchdowns. He's a little guy, he's listed at 5'11" and 170, but he's hardly ever been hurt. His hips are so skinny his back pockets fight each other. But he's wiry and tough, never afraid to go over the middle to catch the slant-in with all those linebackers and safeties trying to break him in two.

Right after Cliff Branch and Dave Dalby helped the Raiders win Super Bowl XI, we got lucky again in the fourth round. Mickey Marvin, a 270-pound guard out of Tennessee, should have been picked earlier, but the scouting reports on him were bad—through no fault of his.

His junior year, Mickey broke an arm. As a senior, he couldn't play in spring practice, he couldn't work out, he couldn't lift weights. About all he could do was eat, which he did very well. Too well. He ballooned up to about three hundred pounds. When the other scouts went to Tennessee, about all they could do was weigh him. When the scale spun up to three hundred pounds, they shook their head and wrote it down. Mickey kept telling those scouts he played at 270, but all those scouts saw was a big fat kid who was overweight. When the other teams passed him up, he was sitting there for us to take in the fourth round.

We had heard that Mickey was a competitor, but we didn't realize how fiery he was until we worked out with the Cowboys at their training camp in Thousand Oaks, just north of Los Angeles.

That year the NFL cut back to only four pre-season games, which are enough for veterans but, as far as I'm concerned, not enough for rookies. I arranged with Tom Landry to bring our younger players down to Thousand Oaks, actually move in with the Cowboys at the Cal Lutheran dorms, and practice against them for a few days.

By the time we got there, I'd heard that Mickey was really fired up, that he hated the Cowboys because their personnel man, Gil Brandt, had predicted that he wasn't much of a prospect. We were just going down to Thousand Oaks to practice, but Mickey was going to World War III.

Our first day there, we had a one-on-one drill—our pass-blockers against the Cowboy pass-rushers. Mickey was our first man up, his eyes blazing through his facemask. I forget who the Cowboy pass-rusher was, but Mickey blasted him, whap, pushed him backwards for maybe five yards.

In his frustration, the Cowboy took a swing at Mickey, who swung back. Mickey was all over him, growling and grunting like my bulldog Boss.

By the time we broke up the fight, Mickey didn't care. He had won his little World War III, his trip to Thousand Oaks had been a success. At lunch that day,

I sat with Dan Reeves, then a Cowboy assistant, who later was hired by the Denver Broncos as head coach.

"In the history of the Dallas Cowboys," he told me, "we've never had an offensive lineman in a fistfight."

Dan loved it. So did I, because I knew our fourth-round choice was a player. By our last day there, I also knew our fifth-round choice that year was a player. Lester Hayes had been a steal that late in the draft. He had been a safety and earlier a linebacker at Texas A. & M., but we projected him as a cornerback. Projected—that's an important word the day of the draft. It means what position a player will fit best on his NFL team, no matter where he played in college. It's a guess. Sometimes you guess wrong. Sometimes you guess right, as we did with Lester Hayes, who at 6' and 200 pounds was bigger than most cornerbacks, but fast and quick. The reason he went so late in the draft was that he had a speech impediment, which some scouts took to mean that he wasn't bright. He was annoyed that he wasn't picked earlier. When he arrived at our rookie camp, he was even annoyed with us for taking him in the fifth round.

"Don't be upset with us," I told him, "we're the team that *did* draft you."

During practice, Lester talked easily. But whenever he had to talk to the coaches or the media, he stammered. Our last day at the Cowboys' camp, we had a game-controlled scrimmage. Around midfield, the Cowboys threw a pass that Lester intercepted. He was running for a touchdown along the far sideline, but just before he got to the end zone, he lifted the ball high in one hand. Just then, a Cowboy tackled him. And he fumbled.

I started running across the field to scream at him, but Lester saw me coming.

"I'll... nnnnnnncver... do it... aaaagain, coach," he said, his arms up. "Nnnnever aaaagain."

He stopped me in my tracks. "Yeah, well, make sure it never happens again," I said. "Just make sure." I turned around and walked back to our sideline. Afterward, Tom Landry and I were talking about the scrimmage.

"You really impressed me, John," he said. "When that kid fumbled and you didn't get mad, you really impressed me."

Little did Tom know how Lester had stopped me from exploding. And that kid developed into an All-Pro cornerback. During the 1980 season, the playoffs and the Raiders' victory in Super Bowl XV, he had a total of 19 interceptions. At the time he was notorious for using stickum on his hands, the same way Fred Biletnikoff did. What most people didn't know was that Lester wasn't using the stickum to hold onto an interception. He used it so that when he bumped a wide receiver with his hands, the wide receiver couldn't escape from his hands. The rule stated that if your hands slipped off the receiver, you couldn't bump him again. All that stickum adhered Lester to the receiver as if he were a big Band-Aid.

After the Raiders won Super Bowl XV, the NFL outlawed stickum. Around that same time Lester got most of the stickum out of his speech. He went to the Communications Resources Center in Roanoke, Virginia, where therapists had him drop his voice level from E pitch to C and monitored his speech patterns with a computerized gadget. Now everybody knows how bright he is.

Maybe the brightest player I ever had was Dave Casper, our second-round choice in 1974 out of Notre Dame, where he had been an All-America tight end as a senior, an offensive tackle as a junior. When he arrived at our rookie minicamp, he weighed 265 pounds. Nobody that big plays tight end. We were projecting him as a guard, maybe a center. But when he reported to training camp, he was down to 220.

"I knew if I came in at 265, you'd make me a lineman," he told me later. "I wanted to play tight end."

Dave graduated from Notre Dame cum laude in economics. After he was traded to the Oilers in 1980, he got high marks in the Houston stockbroker's exam. He got high marks as a tight end too. He could get open, he could catch the ball, and he could block—once I let him play. I made a mistake keeping him behind Bob Moore for two years. The season he took over as the starter, we won Super Bowl XI and he made the All-Pro team. But in practice, sometimes he reverted to being a lineman. If the play went to the other side, he would pull just like a guard—just to make me yell at him. He was always trying to con me. His rookie year, he wobbled into my office with his hip out of joint.

"Hey, go see the doctor," I yelled.

He was double-jointed, that's all. He could do anything with his body, anything with his mind. He was one of the best players I ever had. One of the best friends too. After I stopped coaching, he always phoned me every so often. Even after he was traded to the Oilers in 1980, he kept calling. One night he sounded confused.

"What's the matter?" I asked.

"I want to play guard," he said.

"You dummy, you're still the best tight end in the NFL, stay there."

"All right, I'll stay there."

Another time he phoned to tell me that his wife Sue was pregnant.

"That's great," I said.

"Yeah," he said, "but I don't know what to think."

"You ought to be happy."

"I didn't know," he said.

He had his problems with Eddie Biles, then the Oilers' coach. Eddie had a rule that a player had to keep his helmet on at all times in practice, a rule that Dave didn't agree with. So he wore his helmet when he took a shower. One day in training camp he decided to stay in his room and take a nap instead of having lunch, which broke another rule. Eddie Biles reminded all the players that they had to go to lunch. The next day Dave wore his helmet to lunch, stretched out on a table and took his nap there. After that he always wore his helmet to lunch and ate through his facebars.

In the first round of the draft, teams usually don't project a player. In that round, coaches and scouts like to be sure that a certain player will make their team at a certain position. To be as sure as possible, I always liked to see a player in person whenever I had the opportunity. Over the years the Senior Bowl in Mobile, Alabama, has been the best place for the coaches and scouts to inspect a player. At one time the Senior Bowl was the only all-star game where the coaches were from the NFL or the old AFL staffs. The pro staffs would drill the players at practice in the little things all the other pro coaches wanted to see.

If a defensive lineman is projected as a linebacker in the NFL, the coaches want to see him at linebacker covering a running back on a pass-pattern. They want to see a cornerback covering a wide receiver with good speed. They want to see a quarterback drop back against a strong pass-rush.

After the Raiders lost the 1973 AFC championship game in Miami, I went to Mobile to take a long look at Henry Lawrence of Florida A. & M., a big offensive tackle, 6'4" and 270 pounds. That same year Ed (Too Tall) Jones of Tennessee State, 6'8" and 270, was being talked about as probably the very first choice in the NFL draft. As it turned out, the Cowboys traded Tody Smith and Dave Parks to the Oilers for the first choice, which they used to take Too Tall, who eventually developed into an All-Pro defensive end. At the time of the Senior Bowl, nobody knew which team would get Too Tall, but everybody knew he was good. All the coaches and scouts were watching him go against Henry Lawrence every day in practice.

But the more I watched Too Tall, the more I realized that Henry was blocking him effectively, keeping him away from the passer. After a while, I decided if Henry was blocking the best player in the draft, I wanted Henry.

We took Henry in the first round that year. He developed into one of the NFL's best offensive linemen. He also developed into one of my favorite players. Every year on Thanksgiving when I was the Raiders' coach, I invited any player who didn't have plans to come to our family turkey dinner. Two or three players always stopped by. His rookie year, Henry came over. And he kept coming over on Thanksgiving year after year, even after I stopped coaching. Just before Thanksgiving in 1980, the Raiders lost a tough game in Philadelphia, 10–7, and now Henry was in the midst of his turkey and cranberry sauce when I mentioned that he had some trouble blocking Claude Humphrey, the Eagles' defensive end.

"I know," Henry said. "I didn't think he was that strong."

"You didn't think he was that strong," I exploded. "You never predetermine what a player will be like. You don't play to the level you *think* a player will be at."

I was really hot, pounding the table. The gravy was swaying. The cranberry sauce was jiggling.

"Damn it," I yelled, "you go out there and play to the highest level. You play to be at your best every time, then you won't be fooled by what you *think* the other player is like. When you think he's not that strong or not that quick, it means you're going to take it easy."

Virginia kept eating. She'd heard me before. But our sons Mike and Joe were peeking at Henry, who was staring at his turkey. For a minute or two that Thanksgiving, I was a coach again, bawling out one of my first-round choices. But by the mince pie, I had resumed my retirement.

11

Those Raider
"Renegades"

BEFORE ANY NFL COACH MAKES A TRADE, HE usually checks around with other coaches who know the player involved, especially if he's a player with a past. One day late in our 1976 training camp, George Allen, then coaching the Washington Redskins, phoned me about John Matuszak, a big defensive end then with the Kansas City Chiefs.

"You played against him twice last year," George said. "Is he worth getting?"

"I wouldn't take him, George," I said. "I just don't think he'll help your team."

I'm sure George thought later that I was setting him up—hoping he would ignore "Tooz" so that the Raiders could get him. Or maybe he thought then that I was trying to con him. Whatever, the Redskins traded a 1977 eighth-round choice and a 1978 seventh-round choice to the Chiefs for Tooz, whose value had deteriorated after he had been the very first choice in the

1973 draft. But only a couple of weeks into the 1976 season, George released him. By then, my thinking on Tooz had changed. We had planned to continue using our 4–3 defense that year—four defensive linemen and three linebackers. But injuries had decimated us. Two of our defensive ends, Tony Cline and Horace Jones, and a defensive tackle, Art Thoms, suddenly were out for the season.

Out of necessity, we had to switch to a 3–4 defense. Willie Hall now was our fourth linebacker. But we still needed help at defensive end.

In a 3–4 defense, I've always believed that you need three defensive-tackle types, big guys who can hold their ground, who won't allow themselves to be moved by the offensive push. And that season there weren't many defensive linemen bigger than big Tooz, at 6'7" and 270 pounds the prototype of the bigger, heavier defensive ends you see now.

"What about Matuszak?" Al Davis asked.

"Yeah," I said, "he's worth a shot."

When he arrived, I wasn't about to talk to Tooz about his past. In his travels, every coach and every amateur psychologist had lectured him. He was more experienced at hearing that speech than I was at giving it. He had a reputation as a disruptive influence, but I hadn't phoned George Allen or the coaches in Kansas City and Houston for his report card. Whatever he did that they got rid of him for, if he did it with us, he was gone too. If you know too much about a guy, you tend to pre-judge him, to hold his past against him. I wasn't a psychiatrist or a psychologist. I was a football coach. If you play football for me, good. If you screw up, goodbye.

"I've got three rules," I told him. "Be on time, pay attention, and play like hell when it's time to."

Those rules were for all my players—not just the "renegades," as people liked to call some of them. Yes, the Raiders took a few players that other teams had given up on—not that Al and I thought we had a magic formula to reform them. Our reasoning was, when a player's back is against the wall, when he realizes that no other team wants him, when he knows that the Raiders will be his last stop, that's when he should realize that if he doesn't shape up, his career will be over. We also never gave up much, if anything, to get that type of player. Other teams in every sport make the mistake of trading good players or high draft choices for somebody who has been a problem. But for us, it was always a no-lose situation. If the guy didn't work out, we hadn't lost any important players or draft choices. But some of our renegades really worked out, like Matuszak, who became the left defensive end on our Super Bowl XI team.

I think the only harsh words I ever had with Tooz developed the week after he joined us. We were practicing in the Houston Astrodome on Saturday for our game there the next day.

I was a little edgy. Kenny Stabler was hurt and we had cut George Blanda in training camp. My quarterback suddenly was Mike Rae, who had played in Canada for three years but was a rookie with us. The day before the game I always believed in a long practice. Not hard, but long. I wanted to go through every situation. I wanted my players to be thinking football as long as possible. And having to start Mike Rae meant that we really had to go over everything in the game plan. Finally, we were running short-yardage plays down near the other team's goal-line, which we usually did at the end of Saturday's practice. After a play down there, Tooz looked around at everybody.

"All right," he said, "let's make this last one a good one."

This *last* one. I thought I was the coach. I thought I decided which play would be the last one. I ran over and started screaming at him.

"I'll tell you when the *last* one is," I yelled. "*I'll* tell you, *you* don't tell me."

In the short time Tooz had been with us, he had never seen me explode. As big as he is, he jumped back like he thought I was crazy—which I was, especially with Stabler out. I don't remember how many more plays we ran after that, but it was more than I had originally planned. Quite a few more. The next day, Mike Rae threw two touchdown passes, just enough for us to win, 14–13.

Tooz fit in quickly at left end, next to Dave Rowe at nose tackle and Otis Sistrunk at right end. Like with any new player, I just wanted Tooz to get in the circle with the other players, not try to be a leader. He got in the circle. He was on time, he paid attention, he played like hell when it was time to. And he never again tried to decide which would be the last play in practice.

Otis Sistrunk had arrived in 1972 from the Rams, but beyond that we never had much of a line on him. You know how all NFL players are listed with their names, their position, and their college. Trunk's college was the same as the hair on his head—none. With his shaved head, I had no idea how old he was. For all I knew, he could have been anywhere from twenty-five to forty when we got him. He was a good guy, happy-go-lucky, a fun guy. He always had an answer whenever anybody tried to figure out his age.

"When did you play high school ball?" I once asked him.

"I worked in a factory in high school, coach," he said.

Try to figure that out. But he could play. When we needed a defensive tackle in 1972, I phoned Tommy Prothro, then the Rams' coach. He had just signed Phil Olsen, the younger brother of Merlin Olsen, so we thought the Rams would have to cut one of their defensive tackles.

"That's right, I'll have an extra one," Tommy told me. "Send somebody down to look at them and tell me who you want."

Ron Wolf went down to watch the Rams practice in training camp. That night, he phoned and told me that one of the best defensive tackles there was Otis Sistrunk, but he doubted the Rams would trade him. I figured, hey, take a shot. I phoned Tommy.

"How about that, what's his name, Treetrunk?" I said.

"Sistrunk," he said. "Yeah, we'll let you have him."

We got "Trunk" and a fifth-round draft choice in a trade for our fourth-round choice. He played through the 1979 season, but by then he had an unofficial college. In his first Monday night game as a TV analyst, Alex Karras looked at his monitor showing Trunk on the sideline, the steam rising from his shaved head.

"He's from the University of Mars," Alex said.

Bob Brown, another ex-Ram and known as The Boomer, joined us in a 1971 trade for Kent McCloughan and Harry Schuh after he told the Rams he deserved as much money as Roman Gabriel, their quarterback. Earlier he had been traded by the Eagles when he objected to the firing of Joe Kuharich as general manager.

In his three seasons with us, I never had any trouble with The Boomer—but one of our goal posts did.

When he and the Raider veterans reported to training camp that year, we had two days of meetings before any formal practice. But when the afternoon meeting ended that first day, the veterans and the rookies worked out on their own, running around and throwing the ball. His first day, The Boomer, 6'4" and 280, emerged from the locker room in his black jersey and marched across the field toward the wooden goal posts at the other end. He stopped at one of the goal posts, got down in his three-point stance, put his right foot back for leverage, then put a forearm smash on the goalpost. The goalpost swayed, then toppled backward, the crossbar tipping down. The Boomer had knocked down a *goal post*.

Without a word, he got up and strode back toward his awed teammates. The Boomer had arrived. With a boom.

To strangers, he would introduce himself as Robert Stanford Brown, professional right tackle. But around the team, he just wanted to be called The Boomer. He even called himself that.

"Coach," he told me the day he reported, "The Boomer is here."

Over his career, The Boomer was All-Pro eight times—six times with the Eagles and the Rams, twice with us. Psychologists say that, by nature, offensive linemen are passive people whereas defensive linemen are aggressive. But in personality, The Boomer was more like a defensive tackle. After he arrived, he imposed his personality on some of our best offensive linemen—Art Shell, Gene Upshaw, George Buehler.

"Attack your man, don't let him attack you," he told them. "Always attack."

The Boomer attacked pass-rushers the same way he attacked that wooden goalpost. He had the biggest, strongest arms I've ever seen. He just didn't try to block a pass-rusher, he tried to punch a pass-rusher, preferably in the solar plexus where there's no protective equipment. After one of those punches, the guy he was blocking puked right there on the field. Even in practice, The Boomer didn't want to be beaten. When he was with the Rams, he had some tremendous battles with Deacon Jones, their Hall of Fame defensive end, on the practice field. In those years, the rules permitted a pass-rusher to head-slap a pass-blocker, whack him across the helmet. I don't know if Deacon invented the head-slap, but he popularized it. Except that The Boomer didn't like it.

"Don't do it anymore," The Boomer told him time after time. "I'm warning you, don't do it anymore."

Deacon just laughed. Until the day he swatted The Boomer and realized his left hand was impaled on The Boomer's helmet. On each side of a helmet, a small padded screw holds the inner cushion. The Boomer had replaced one of these screws with a longer screw that had been sharpened like an ice pick. As soon as Deacon slapped The Boomer's helmet, his hand was stuck on that sharpened screw. Howling, he stared at his bloody hand.

"What the hell's that on your helmet?" Deacon screamed.

"I warned you not to do it anymore," The Boomer said.

Deacon never did it anymore, at least not to The Boomer in practice. To this day, Deacon has a big scar in the middle of his left hand. I know nobody slapped The Boomer around in our practices. He was not only one of the toughest players I've ever known, but also one of the smartest. Not just football-smart either. As an All-America guard at Nebraska, he earned a bachelor of science degree in biology. Even before he joined the Eagles as their first-round draft choice, he enrolled at the University of Pennsylvania and later got a master's degree in education administration.

Bob Brown was nobody's fool, and nobody to fool with. He has settled in Oakland, so I see him every so often. He still works out and lifts weights every day. He's still The Boomer.

The season we won Super Bowl XI, we picked up Carl Garrett from the Jets for a tenth-round draft choice. Not much of a price for a running back who rushed for 220 yards on only 48 carries, an excellent 4.6 average. Playing behind Clarence Davis in the Super Bowl, he had a 13-yard run to the Viking 13 that led to our first touchdown. When we got him, I remembered I had tried to scout him on a spring trip in 1968 when he was at New Mexico Highlands. The day I got there, I went to practice to see him.

"Which one is Garrett?" I asked.

"He's not here," somebody said.

"What's wrong? Is he injured?"

"No, he doesn't like spring practice. He only shows up if he feels like it."

"Oh," I said. "One of those."

But in the fall he obviously felt like playing. He rushed for 3,862 yards in three seasons there. As the Patriots' third-round choice in 1969, he was voted the

AFL's rookie of the year over O.J. Simpson, the very first choice that year as the Heisman Trophy winner. Four years later Carl was traded to the Bears for a first-round choice, then he drifted to the Jets in 1975 for Mike Adamle and a fourth-round choice.

But when we got him, we didn't care why he had been traded so often. In those years some teams might trade a player if he didn't wear a necktie on a trip. No matter what it was, Carl started fresh with us. And he gave us a big year.

As good as he was, though, Carl Garrett was never really a Raider to the other veterans. That's true of anybody who joins your team after he's been with a few other teams.

The season we won Super Bowl XI, we also had Ted Kwalick, once an All-Pro tight end with the 49ers, who had jumped to the World Football League before we signed him as Dave Casper's backup. He hung out with our players. That wasn't the problem. But he had been such a good player with the 49ers and now he wasn't really that good for us. If you watched him closely, you saw he was still a 49er tight end. Our tight end had to be a really good blocker; he wasn't a good blocker. Our tight end had to run disciplined square-out and comeback pass-patterns; he had always been more of a freelance pass-receiver.

It works the other way too. As great a tight end as Dave Casper was with the Raiders, after he was traded to the Oilers in 1979, he has never been that good again. To me, he was a Raider tight end playing for Houston, just as Ted Kwalick had been a 49er tight end playing for Oakland.

For all their talent, you learn as a coach not to rely on new older players as *your* players. The ones you rely on must be those who grew up with your organization. The more of those players you have, the better your team is. That's one reason the Steelers, the Cowboys, the Dolphins, and lately the Redskins have been so successful. It's easy to look at a player on another team and think, *I'd love to have that guy, he'd be great with us,* but it doesn't always work out. You can never be sure of that guy being as good or better than he was on another team.

Young players from other teams sometimes fit in quickly. Daryle Lamonica hadn't played much in Buffalo, he hadn't established himself as a *Bill,* so he was able to be a *Raider* almost immediately. For his first five seasons, Ted Hendricks had been with the Colts and the Packers, so it took him a little more time before he felt like a *Raider,* before the other players accepted him as a *Raider.*

Warren Wells, a wide receiver who had too short and too sad a career, was another young player who became a Raider quickly after having bounced around. I had several great players but Warren may have been the most talented of them all. He could run like a deer. He could catch the ball. He could block. He could tackle on special teams. And he was my son Mike's favorite player. Mike was just a little kid when Warren used to give him gum and talk to him. I have a picture of Mike sitting on Warren's lap. And wherever Mike has played football, he has always worn Warren's number, eighty-one, if it was available. One day after Mike had gotten to know Warren, a friend of ours who didn't know Warren asked Mike about him.

"Is he white or black?" our friend said.

Mike thought and said, "I don't know."

Warren had been with the Lions in 1964 before

spending two years in Alaska in the army. After his discharge, the Lions cut him and the Chiefs were looking at him at training camp in 1967 when we spotted him while watching a film of an exhibition game. At the time Otis Taylor was the Chiefs' best wide receiver. We were watching this film when one of the Chiefs wide receivers made a big play.

"Otis Taylor," I said, "is really tough."

"He sure is," Ron Wolf, our personnel director, said. "Hey, that's not Taylor, that's not eighty-nine."

"Who is it then?"

Checking the Chiefs' roster, we found out that Warren Wells had made that catch. Several days later Al Davis got a phone call from Lloyd Wells, a scout for the Chiefs who was not related to Warren but who had known him at Texas Southern.

"Lloyd told me the Chiefs are going to cut that kid you saw on film," Al told the coaches. "I think we'll sign him for the special teams and work with him as a receiver."

As great a wide receiver as he turned out to be, Warren was also the best special-teams player I ever had. Covering kickoffs or punts, he had a way of snaking through to make the tackle. Nobody could block him. His instincts were amazing. And he was even better as a receiver. Of the 13 passes he caught as a rookie, 6 were for touchdowns. The next year, he caught 53 passes for 1,137 yards and 11 touchdowns; in 1969, he caught 47 for 1,260 yards (an incredible 26.8-yard average) and 14 touchdowns before a shoulder injury knocked him out of the playoffs; in 1970 he caught 43 passes for 935 yards and 11 touchdowns.

One of those 1970 touchdowns came on the most amazing catch I've ever seen. We were playing the

Jets at Shea Stadium, trailing 13–6, with 28 seconds left when we got the ball at our own 30-yard line. On first down, Warren drew a pass-interference penalty against Earlie Thomas, the cornerback who was covering him. Now we were on the Jets' 33 with 22 seconds.

After two incompletions, only eight seconds were on the clock. Lamonica dropped back and threw a pass into the left corner of the end zone where Warren was surrounded by Thomas and W. K. Hicks, a Jet safety. From where I was standing along the sideline, I saw the ball pop up in the air as if Warren had bobbled it. Next thing I knew, Warren had caught it for a touchdown with :01 showing on the clock. George Blanda kicked the extra point and we won, 14–13.

On our game film the next day, it still looked as if Warren had bobbled the ball. The next spring when we got our Raider highlight film that NFL Films produces, we saw that one of their cameramen had a shot that showed Warren reaching between the two Jets, tipping the ball away from them, and then catching it as he fell to the ground. Damndest catch I've ever seen.

But in 1971 he didn't play. He would never play again. Back in 1969 he had pleaded guilty in Oakland to a charge of attempted rape. He was put on three years' probation, which required him to stay out of bars. Warren couldn't drink. Not that he drank a lot. But after one drink, some of my players told me, Warren was a different person. He had several other problems with the police—drunken driving, carrying a concealed weapon. Then shortly before he was to report to training camp in 1971, he was stabbed by a woman in Beaumont, Texas, his hometown. In a bar. That revoked his probation. He did ten months in confinement, some of it in state prisons, before a judge ordered him to a Synanon commune at Santa Monica in what had once been an expensive hotel. Some of the inmates were living there with their wives and kids, but Warren was alone. Warren was always alone. His marriage had broken up. He had nobody.

"I'm making the best of it," he told me when I visited him. "I'll be ready for training camp."

But when he arrived at training camp in 1972, he was a totally different athlete. He was running in slow motion. At first I thought he was just taking it easy to avoid pulling a muscle. But as the exhibition games approached, I decided that he had to speed up. I wanted him to start showing me the Warren Wells that I had to see, the Warren Wells who always had thrived on great one-on-one duels with Willie Brown in practice.

"It's time," I told him, "to kick it into high gear. Let's see you really run."

Warren nodded and lined up for a deep post pattern. But when he took off, he was still running in slow motion. On his way back, I walked over to him again.

"That's not your high gear," I said.

"Yeah," he said. "I was really moving."

Whatever had happened to him in that year off, Warren was running as fast as he could, but it was nowhere near fast enough. I had to cut him, and it was as tough a cut as I've ever made. I think I worried about it more than he did. The day I told him, he didn't seem to mind.

"That's all right, coach," he said. "You gave me my shot."

I don't know why or how, but Warren had changed in that year off. Physically, his whole system had slowed down. Mentally, he was placid, passive. He had lost his drive, lost his desire. And his problems had just begun. In 1976, in Beaumont, he was arrested for attempted robbery of a woman outside a Houston supermarket. He later was sentenced to three years at Huntsville, a maximum-security prison. He was still there when Al Davis organized a Raider alumni reunion. As the Raider director of special projects, I was in charge of contacting all our former players.

"I know Warren's in jail," Al said, "but I want him here. Tell those prison people the Raiders will pay all the expenses for Warren and as many guards as they want to send with him."

But the Huntsville warden wouldn't let Warren leave. The last I heard, he was in Houston, trying to make a go of his life. I've always thought that his problem in Oakland was being single. After practice, a single player is on his own. He has no wife and kids to go home to, only an empty apartment or hotel room. So a single player tends to go to bars, stay out late, not eat right, not get enough sleep.

"If you've got a nice girl, get married," I used to tell my single players. "Buy a house, get a station wagon, a dog, and a lawn-mower."

When they see me, confirmed bachelors like Clarence Davis, George Atkinson, and Tom Keating still laugh about that little speech. But they were able to handle being single. Warren wasn't. Even when Warren tried to do the right thing, it backfired.

"You can't play this game forever," I once told him. "If you build a good reputation, you'll have an opportunity to do something solid with your life. Get involved with the community."

Not long after that Warren visited some kids at a local hospital. When he told me one little kid in particular had really enjoyed seeing him, I thought of how Warren was my son Mike's favorite player. I thought Warren had really found something to do with his spare time, especially when he showed me a big get-well card he had bought for the kid at the hospital.

"I'm going to get all the players to autograph it," he said. "He'll love it."

In the locker room that day, Warren handed the card to some of the players and asked them to write something nice on it for the little kid who was in the hospital. Our players were always autographing cards like that. But some of them couldn't believe Warren had gone to see a little kid in a hospital.

"This isn't for some kid," I heard one of the players say. "This must be for some chick Warren is trying to impress."

I didn't think anything of it at the time but a few minutes later I happened to be standing near Warren when the card made its way back to him. Instead of wishing the kid a quick recovery, some of the players had written obscene phrases on the card. As soon as Warren read what was on the card, he tore it up. I can still see the pieces of that card falling to the floor.

As far as I know, Warren never went back to see that little kid in the hospital.

12

The Super Hoopla

BY THE TIME I GOT TO SUPER BOWL XI AS A head coach, I knew how to handle it. Not the game. Hell, a football game is a football game—that's the easy part. The most important thing for a coach to know about the Super Bowl is how to handle the hoopla.

I think I learned that at the Pro Bowl, of all places. After the NFL's merger and realignment into two conferences in 1970, I coached the AFC team in four of the next six Pro Bowl games. I coached it again after the 1977 season. Which sounds terrific. Hey, he coached the Pro Bowl five times. That's a lot better than having people say, hey, he lost more AFC championship games than anybody else. Because that's how you get to coach the Pro Bowl, by losing your conference championship game. When we were losing so many of them, some people were saying that the Raiders and I couldn't win the "big one." But those people just waited until we finally lost each season, then they called that game the big one. What they forgot is that we had to win several big ones to get to the conference championship game. Hey, tell me what the big one is *before* we play it, not after. Then we'll count up how many we win and how many we don't. But by listening all those years to my Pro Bowl players talk about their Super Bowl experiences, I got to know what, for a coach, was right or wrong.

"Imagine that," I remember Jake Scott of the Dolphins bitching one year, "the other players could bring their wives, but I couldn't bring my mother."

At Super Bowl VIII in Houston, the Dolphin policy was that the club would arrange for the married players' wives to come there on a chartered jet and stay at another hotel, but it ignored the unmarried players. The idea, I guess, was to avoid having girlfriends along, but the Dolphins hadn't thought about Jake's mother.

"If the club takes the wives," Jake kept grumbling, "it should take my mother."

At the Pro Bowl that year I was hanging out with my AFC players at our hotel meeting room where I always had coffee and rolls for them in the morning. Psychiatrists call that "communicating" with players, but I prefer to call it "hanging out." My first four years as the Pro Bowl coach, we had several players from the AFC teams that had just won the Super Bowl— the 1970 Colts, the 1973 Dolphins, the 1974 and 1975 Steelers. I was hanging out with guys who knew what they liked and what they didn't like about the Super Bowl, guys who knew what they thought was important and unimportant.

Every year some players would talk about "distractions," using the word that George Allen popularized when the Redskins lost Super Bowl VII to the Dolphins, 14–7. The more those players talked, the more I realized that their distractions had nothing to do with football or even football practice. All their distractions involved the hoopla—tickets, travel arrangements, and hotel rooms for their families and friends, and the news media. And it seemed to me that the teams that complained the most about distractions had lost—the Redskins at Super Bowl VII, the Vikings at Super Bowl VIII.

When the Raiders lost Super Bowl II to the Packers, 33–14, I was a rookie assistant coach, but at that time there wasn't nearly so much hoopla. Nobody took the AFL or the Super Bowl seriously until Joe Namath and the Jets stung the Colts, 16–7, the next year.

But from the start I always thought the Super Bowl is an unnatural game—an empty week, then a second week at a strange hotel and an unfamiliar practice complex, wives and families and friends arriving the weekend of the game. Those things don't happen during the season or even during the playoffs. But with a little planning, you can make the Super Bowl seem like it's almost natural. As soon as my Raiders beat the Steelers in the 1976 AFC championship game, I knew how I wanted to handle our Super Bowl preparations— by using that first week to head off as many distractions as possible.

"Tickets," I told my players at our first meeting that week, "you each get to buy thirty tickets but I suggest you get rid of them before we go to L.A. next week. That way, nobody will be bothering you next week about tickets. If you don't have any, you don't have any."

As the coach, I think I had fifty tickets, but I never

got involved with them. I didn't want to get involved with them. The day I got my tickets, I took them home and handed them to Virginia and told her, "You know our friends who should get these better than I do." Virginia took it from there. That was one distraction I didn't have to deal with, maybe the biggest distraction.

"Now for hotel rooms," I told the players. "In addition to your room at the team hotel, we'll arrange for a 'guest' of your choice to go to L.A. on our front-office charter that weekend and have a room at the hotel in L.A. where our front-office people will be staying."

As for the media schedule, I had to go along with what the commissioner's office had arranged. But it wasn't as complex as I had feared it might be. I knew the TV cameras would be at the airport when we arrived Monday, but other than that, the NFL had everything organized. Tuesday would be photo day, with all our players in uniform out on the field at the University of California at Irvine before our practice. Wednesday morning and Thursday morning I had to hold a news conference in the ballroom at the Newport Beach Marriott where we were staying, followed by the players' individual news conferences, one at each table in the ballroom. Friday morning I had to go up to the NFL headquarters, the Marriott near the Los Angeles airport, for another news conference. The surroundings and the schedule had improved from Super Bowl II in Miami when we stayed in a bleak motel up near Boca Raton and the writers piled out of station wagons at any hour for their interviews.

"Other than what's on the schedule," Don Weiss, the NFL's executive director, told me, "you and your players don't have to do any other media conferences. If it's not on that schedule, you don't have to do it."

That first week, I told the players about the media schedule so it wouldn't come as a surprise at Newport Beach when we got there. Anytime there's a surprise, it's a distraction. The two days they had to be in the ballroom at the Newport Beach Marriott for their individual news conferences, I told them to sit at the table marked with their uniform number.

"You're going to get more publicity than you ever have in your life," I told them. "Enjoy it."

I worried that some of our little-known players would be sitting at their tables all by themselves, with nobody interviewing them. But as far as I could tell, that didn't happen. There's usually a writer from that guy's hometown area or from his college area who wants to get the local angle.

With all those possible "distractions" taken care of, all we had to do now was get ready for the Vikings, for the game.

In other years, some Super Bowl teams had used that empty week to put in their game plan. But we didn't. We just showed our players films of the Vikings in order to familiarize them with the players they would be going against. If we had put in our game plan that early, I thought the players might be bored with it by the second week. This way, when we put it in the week before the game like we always do, they were eager for it. Our game plan wasn't fancy or tricky. We just didn't want to be predictable. We wanted to run on passing downs, to pass on running downs, to run on running downs, to pass on passing downs. We wanted not to get into any regular pattern. But no matter how big a game it is, Wednesday and Thursday are your most important practice days. With us, Wednesday was always defensive day, Thursday offensive day. But that Wednesday, too many of our players didn't seem to be concentrating. Now that I look back, maybe I was just looking for a reason to jump on them. But when somebody blew a coverage, I started yelling.

"Hold it, hold it," I roared. "Over here, everybody over here."

Right there in the middle of the field I reminded them that to win the Super Bowl, they had to concentrate now. Not just on Sunday, but now. I reminded them that they couldn't be thinking about things outside of football.

"You've got the whole rest of your life," I roared, "to think about things outside of football."

That night I worried that, by trying to avoid the distractions, maybe I had distracted them. When it was raining Thursday when I woke up, then I worried even more. The worst type of day to practice is a rainy day. In the rain, somebody can slip and pull a groin or a hamstring. In the rain, footballs get wet and your quarterback can hurt his arm throwing those heavy balls. As soon as I saw the rain that morning, I told my equipment man, Dick Romanski, to buy three dozen footballs.

"But we've got three dozen now," Dick told me.

"I know, but I want a dry ball *every play*."

This wasn't the usual warm rain you get in California—this was a cold rain that chilled you to the bone. But that day Ken Stabler had the best practice I've ever seen a quarterback have. We threw what we called "individual"—him throwing to his receivers without any coverage. We threw "one on one," with one defensive back covering one receiver. We threw what we called "skeleton," seven against seven (without four offensive linemen and the four defensive linemen). And we threw "team," the entire eleven on offense against the entire eleven on defense.

For about two hours, Kenny threw over a hundred passes, and only *one* ball hit the ground. He completed every pass he threw except one across the field to Dave Casper—who should have caught it, but he put only one hand up and didn't hold onto it.

One incompletion in two hours. I had never seen anything like that. It made me feel a little better. And on Friday, the whole team was sharp. Kenny was still sharp, the defense was sharp, the special teams were sharp. Walking off the field by myself, I thought, *You got it now, just don't screw it up!* I decided to pull in my horns and stop coaching. I normally don't believe that the hay is in the barn. I think you coach your team all the way up to and through the game. But the whole team had been so sharp Friday after Kenny had been so sharp the day before that I didn't want to disrupt them in any way. Sometimes on a Saturday you'll put in a new play. But if I had put in a new play that Saturday, all I could have done was screw up what I had. And what I had was a team that *I knew* was going to win the Super Bowl.

"We're going to kill 'em," I told Al Davis the night before the game, "I just know we're going to kill 'em tomorrow."

"No, no, John, don't talk like that," Al said. "Don't ever talk like that before a game, you know better than that."

After practice that Saturday, the team had moved up to the L.A. Hilton, with Al's help. Newport Beach was fine for practice, but we realized that on Sunday morning it would take us anywhere from two to three hours to bus up the freeways to the Rose Bowl in

Pasadena, where Super Bowl XI would be played. Jim Otto, our Hall of Fame center and our business manager that season, tried to find another hotel, but all of them were booked.

"This is a serious problem," I told Al. "We've got to find a hotel either in Pasadena or L.A."

Al just looked at me. "Have you tried Barron?" he said, meaning Barron Hilton, the chairman of the Hilton chain. In the AFL's early years, Barron owned the San Diego Chargers and he's still a minority owner.

"Jim doesn't know Barron," I said.

"I'll call Barron myself," Al said.

Suddenly we had rooms in the L.A. Hilton for Saturday night. But now I had another idea that my Daly City pal, John Robinson, now the Rams' coach, had suggested. The season before John took the Southern Cal job, he had been one of my Raider assistants. The day he left, he made a prediction.

"Next year," he said, "I'm going to be in the Rose Bowl with SC and you're going to be in the Super Bowl at the Rose Bowl with the Raiders, you wait and see."

It worked out just that way. John's team beat Michigan in the Rose Bowl, 14–6, and now I was getting my Raiders ready to play there. Two guys from Daly City who had hitchhiked over to St. Mary's College to see the 49ers with Frankie Albert and Hugh McElhenny in training camp, who had sneaked into NFL games at Kezar Stadium and into Pacific Coast League baseball games at Seals Stadium, who were always playing ball together. One time John got a new Louisville Slugger, a black bat that cost $3.75, a fortune to us then.

"Let me swing it," I said.

"No, no," he said. "Nobody's going to swing this bat until I bone it."

"Until you what?"

"Rub a ham bone on it like the real ballplayers do," he said. "It hardens the wood."

"Yeah, right."

John boned that bat for weeks. All the while he wouldn't let anybody touch it, much less swing it. Finally at Marchbank Park where we played baseball, he decided to use it in a game. His first swing, craaaaack, the bat split. I didn't know whether to laugh or cry, so I laughed. We always laughed.

The guys in our neighborhood had a deal where if, say, I bought a candy bar, and John yelled "bites" before I yelled "no bites," I had to give him a bite. The trick was, if another guy yelled "bites" first, you'd spit on your candy bar. All the other guys would turn away muttering, but John still took his bite. Finally, one summer when my mother offered me twenty-five dollars to paint our back porch, I got John good.

"You want to make some money?" I asked him.

"Yeah," he said. "I really need some cash."

"My mother asked me to paint our back porch but I'm real busy. If you do it, I'll pay you ten dollars."

"You got a deal," he said.

I slipped the other fifteen dollars in my pocket.

Now here we were, two guys from Daly City coaching teams who were playing in the Rose Bowl stadium about a week apart. I phoned John to find out if there was anything about the Rose Bowl field I should know.

"The field is fine," he said. "It's getting to the field that's the problem. Once you get off the freeway, you go through all these little streets in a residential area.

You need a helicopter to lead your buses through those streets."

Good idea. My mistake was trying to improve on it. I figured if a college team needed one helicopter, an NFL team ought to have two. One in front of the buses, one behind the buses. I didn't really think about it again until I was riding to the Rose Bowl that Sunday morning on one of our three chartered buses. I looked up at our lead helicopter guiding us and then I glanced back at the other helicopter behind us.

How dumb can you be? I told myself. *You've got one helicopter up there telling us where to go and another helicopter in back telling us where we've been.*

By then, I had a real problem. I always wanted my team to be at the stadium two hours before gametime. With a 12:30 kickoff, I originally told the players we would leave the hotel at 10 o'clock, but at the pregame meal that morning I announced that the buses would leave at 9:45, then I moved it up to 9:30 instead. Without realizing it, I had broken one of my Super Bowl commandments—no surprises. By 9 o'clock, I was so edgy, I was out on the sidewalk, ready to go. Some of my players were with me, along with several fans. One of the fans was wearing a pirate costume that resembled the Raider logo. When he saw me standing there on the sidewalk, he came over.

"How about letting me be your mascot today?" he said.

"No, we don't need a mascot," I said. "No mascot."

In the confusion, I looked around at the players and yelled, "Time to go, let's go, let's get on the buses." In a few minutes, we were on our way, but I just knew something was wrong. I glanced at my watch. It was only 9:15, which meant we must have left at 9:10.

Oh, oh, I told myself, *we've left some players back at the hotel. And it's my fault, not theirs.*

As soon as we got into our locker room, I started looking around to see who was missing. I could tell by their empty lockers that Clarence Davis, John Matuszak, Carl Garrett, and Hubie Ginn were not there. Now what do I do—send a helicopter back? No, that's silly, a helicopter couldn't land near the hotel. Maybe a police car. Yeah, a police car. You dummy, you're in the Super Bowl and you left four players at the hotel.

Sooner or later, I knew I had to tell somebody. I barged into the trainer's room where George Anderson was.

"George, I think I left four players at the hotel," I said. "I told the buses to leave earlier than the scheduled time. Four players are still back at the hotel, George, we've got to get a police car to go get 'em."

"They're here," George said.

"They're not here," I said. "I've been looking all over this locker room and they're not here."

"Yes, they are," George said.

"How'd they get here then?"

"That guy in the pirate costume, he drove two of 'em out and the other two took a cab."

"Where are they now?"

"They're hiding," George said. "They thought they were late. They thought you'd chew them out and fine them."

"No fine," I said. "Tell them no fine."

If anything, I should have fined myself. But just knowing that all my players were there, I started to feel good again about the game—until it was time for introductions. I got a little edgy then, especially when

Joe Browne of the NFL office started to organize our players for the introductions.

"When I call out..." Joe started to say.

"I don't want you talking to my team," I said. "*I'll* tell my players what order to go out there in, not you."

"All right, coach," Joe said.

But when it was time for the actual introductions, Joe checked his watch.

"All right, Raiders," he said.

"Hey, I told you to keep quiet," I said. "Don't you talk to my football team. I'll do this."

"Sorry, coach," he said.

But when I ran out there into the Rose Bowl and saw 100,421 people, I started to feel better. We won the toss, took the kickoff, and drove to the Vikings' 21-yard line before Errol Mann's 29-yard field-goal attempt hit the left upright. The next time we got the ball, we had to punt from our 39, but I wasn't concerned.

When we had to punt the third time we had the ball, I also wasn't concerned, but I should have been.

Ray Guy was not only the NFL's best punter but in his four seasons he had never had a punt blocked. Never. So when Ray went back to punt, I wasn't even paying attention. About five minutes were left in the first quarter with no score, and I was talking to Kenny Stabler. Ray was waiting on our 19 for the snap.

Instead of hearing the *boom* of his punt, I suddenly heard the *blap* that means only one thing. His punt had been blocked.

When a punt is blocked, three things can happen— all of them bad. One, the ball can still go forward a few yards. Two, it can fall straight down. Three, it can go backward—which is the worst thing that can happen, especially when you're not that far from your own end zone. This blocked punt went backward, all the way to our 3-yard line where a Viking linebacker, Fred McNeil, fell on it.

As our defense hurried onto the field, I remembered how I had told Al that I was so sure we were going to win and I remembered how he told me, "Don't ever talk like that, John, you know better than to talk like that." I did know better.

On first down Chuck Foreman got a yard to our 2, but on second down, Phil Villapiano hit Brent McClanahan, who fumbled. Willie Hall recovered on the 1 for us. That good feeling came over me again. Our defense hurried off the field, jumping and yelling, slapping hands and hugging each other, proving my theory that success breeds togetherness, not that togetherness breeds success. When players do well, they all love each other. When they play badly, they hardly look at each other. But in the jubilation of the fumble recovery, Jack Tatum hurried over to me and nodded toward Villapiano.

"You better check out Phil," he said.

"What's the matter with him?" I asked.

"I think he's goofy," Jack told me.

"He's always a little goofy," I said.

"No, he's more goofy than usual," Jack said. "When we were in our huddle down there near the goal-line, he was saying, 'Now we got 'em where we want 'em.'"

"He said that?"

"He said that."

I walked over to where Phil was sitting on the bench. "You all right?" I asked.

"Yeah, I'm fine," he said.

"The guys told me you were saying, 'Now we got 'em where we want 'em.'"

"We did have 'em where we want 'em."

"We did? On our 3 . . . on our 2?"

"Yeah. Down there, they couldn't throw any deep passes, they weren't going to run any sweeps or any reverses, they were just going to run up the middle. I got in there, the ball popped loose, and we got it. We had 'em right where we wanted 'em."

"Yeah, you're right," I said. "Yeah, we did have 'em right where we wanted 'em."

Phil Villapiano was like that. To me, there are three types of people, whether they are football players or not. People who make things happen. People who watch things happen. And people who don't know what's happening. Phil makes things happen. He had a linebacker's personality, he loved to hit—like Dick Butkus did, like Lawrence Taylor does. Believe me, not many guys really love to hit, but Phil did. And when he hit Brent McClanahan, he turned Super Bowl XI around.

On third down, Clarence Davis went off left tackle for 35 yards to our 41 early in the second quarter, then we drove to the Vikings' 7 before we had to settle for a 24-yard field goal. On the sideline our offensive unit was happy but I was screaming, "You got to finish 'em off, you got to get the ball in the end zone, you got to get six points, not three." Kenny Stabler put his arm around me.

"Don't worry, John," he said, "there's plenty more where that came from."

I reacted like a baby who is crying and has a pacifier stuck in his mouth. I shut up. Kenny was right. Our next possession, he ended a 64-yard drive with a 1-yard pass to Dave Casper in the end zone. Our following possession, he hit Fred Biletnikoff for 17 yards to their 1-yard line and Pete Banaszak scored on the next play. Even though Erroll Mann's extra point was wide, we were ahead at halftime, 16–0, really in control. In the third quarter Erroll kicked a 40-yard field goal before the Vikings finally scored on Fran Tarkenton's 8-yard pass to Sammy White.

In the final quarter, the Vikings were driving again when Willie Hall intercepted at our 30 and ran it back to our 46. On third down, Kenny hit Fred Biletnikoff for a 48-yard gain to the 2 and Pete Banaszak went over right tackle on the next play. We were ahead, 26–7, and the Vikings were desperate. Tarkenton was passing on every play when Willie Brown picked one off at our 25 and raced down the other sideline for a touchdown. We were ahead, 32–7, with less than 6 minutes left. I knew we had won. Call in the dogs and piss on the fire!

The final was 32–14. The Vikings scored in the last minute on a 13-yard pass from their backup quarterback, Bob Lee, to Stu Voight, but I never saw it. I was too busy celebrating on the sideline, walking up and down and shaking hands. Kenny Stabler had completed 12 of 19 passes for 180 yards. Fred Biletnikoff had caught 4 for 79 yards, Dave Casper 4 for 70 yards. Clarence Davis had carried 16 times for 137 yards. Our defense had limited the Vikings to only 86 yards of total offense in the first half—when the game was really decided. Now, after the gun went off ending the game, my three tallest players—John Matuszak, Ted Hendricks, and Charles Philyaw—were carrying me off the field on their shoulders when one of them tripped over a photographer in front of us.

One by one, Tooz, Ted, and Charles went down in a heap and I went down on top of them. That's the picture *The New York Times* used on its front page the next day.

I didn't get hurt. At that moment, I could've fallen on my head on cement and not been hurt. I hurried to my feet and ran into our locker room.

"Great game," I told the players. "We're the champions. This is what it's all about."

They cheered, I cheered. Then somebody from the NFL office was hurrying me outside to where the media had assembled for interviews. I answered questions for more than half an hour. On the way back into the dressing room, I heard one of my players shouting at me.

"The ring, Coach," he was saying. "We got the ring!"

He meant the Super Bowl ring that Al Davis, his executive assistant Al LoCasale, and I would design— "Oakland Raiders" and "World Champions" above and below a full-carat diamond surrounded by 16 five-point diamonds in the shape of a football, five more five-point diamonds on each side of the face, the word "pride" and the scores of both Super Bowl XI and the AFC championship game on one side of the ring, "poise" and the person's name and position or title on the other side. But the "A" standing for the AFC is the thin "A" from the old AFL insignia, not the thicker, block "A" of the AFC emblem. We all wanted that link to our AFL roots.

In the AFL, we had been looked down upon by the NFL as second-rate teams. When the Jets won Super Bowl III, it gave us equality. But even after the 1970 realignment, I always got a little more pleasure out of beating the old NFL teams.

When we played the Broncos in Denver for the 1977 AFC championship, it bothered me to see the red-white-and-blue NFL shield painted across the fifty-yard line. For two original AFL teams, that logo just didn't play. That's why we put the thin "A" from the old AFL logo on our Super Bowl ring.

In my office after winning Super Bowl XI that day, I looked up and saw John Robinson holding a bottle of champagne. I hadn't seen him all day but here he was, reminding me how he had predicted his Southern Cal team would win the Rose Bowl game in the Rose Bowl and how my Raiders would win the Super Bowl game in the Rose Bowl about a week later. Here we were, two guys from Daly City who grew up together. I had my first beer with John Robinson—and now I was drinking champagne with him in the Rose Bowl locker room after the biggest week in our lives. My boys Mike and Joe were there too, waiting for me to change my clothes.

"Hey, nobody can say your dad can't win the big one anymore," I told them. "Not anymore."

13

My Fair Advantage

PART OF THE FUN OF COACHING IS THE OTHER coaches. At an NFL meeting once, we were trying to come up with a precise definition for legal pass protection, as opposed to holding. After a while, Weeb Ewbank, who was coaching the Jets then, put on his best sincere look. His offensive linemen were some of the most notorious holders in the NFL, but Weeb was all innocence.

"We have to get this defined so we can coach it," Weeb said. "I just want my fair advantage."

That *fair advantage* is all any coach ever wants, physically or psychologically. One Saturday before a big game with the Kansas City Chiefs, I noticed some workmen at the Oakland Coliseum going in and out of the visiting team's locker room.

"What are you guys doing?" I asked.

"We're exterminators," the boss said. "We were told

a couple of rats have been seen in the visitors' locker room."

"You serious?" I asked.

"Dead serious," he said.

"Come back Monday and get rid of them," I said. "Monday is plenty of time."

"We're supposed to do it today."

"No, no, you have my permission to leave now and come back Monday morning," I said. "Leave the rats in there. Throw some food in there for 'em. Just wait until Monday to get rid of 'em."

"If you say so, coach," the boss said.

Even without rats in the locker room, Oakland was a hard place to play for a visiting team. Coming in, they had to walk through a dingy, damp, gray hallway and then go down some gray stairs into the bowels of the stadium. The visiting team's locker room was partitioned into a series of small rooms, so they never had the feeling of being together. They also knew that as soon as they emerged out of another dingy tunnel onto the field, they would be booed unmercifully. Oakland was not a fun place to play, especially for Hank Stram and the Chiefs, one of our biggest rivals then. As soon as the Chiefs were settled in their locker room Sunday morning, I knocked on the door. One of their equipment men answered.

"I have to talk to Hank," I said.

Hank appeared, dapper as always, a red vest under his black blazer. Behind him, the locker room was hushed as it always is before a game, but I didn't invite Hank out into the hallway to talk. I wanted him to stand there with the door open so some of his players could hear me.

"We've got a problem," I said loudly. "Some *rats* have

been seen in this locker room. We've got exterminators working on it but some *rats* might still be around. Just to be safe, Hank, you better warn your players about the *rats*."

Every time I used the word rats, I could see some players looking around. I had established my fair advantage. I don't know if it helped, but it didn't hurt. We won the game.

At the Pro Bowl after that season, Willie Lanier of the Chiefs told me how his teammates had been squirming around in the locker room, checking their shoes and their shoulder pads. Some even peered into their helmets before putting them on. I always liked to put something in Hank's mind. Before another game in Oakland we were out on the field, which was actually below sea level. If there was any rain at all, the water table would rise and the grass would be slick. That week it had rained enough for me to give Hank something to think about.

"You won't believe this, Hank," I said. "Yesterday I told the groundskeeper to put two hours of water on the field. But after he turned the water on, he took a lunch break and fell asleep. The water was on for eight hours. I'm really sorry about this, Hank, but your receivers can work around where it's really wet."

Hank stormed off, but not before I had wished him good luck, which he hated to hear. Most coaches don't want the opposing coach to wish them good luck, because then they have to wish the opposing coach good luck, which they don't want to do. Most coaches think that if they have to wish you good luck, then you *will* have good luck and win. I didn't care. I knew that wishing the other coach good luck had nothing to do with winning or losing the game. But if you wish most coaches good luck, they grudgingly wish you the same.

"Yeah, good luck," Hank would always say quickly, his voice dropping. "Yeah, yeah, good luck."

Anything to get the other coach thinking negatively. But there were times when Hank got me too. Hank had a team chaplain, Monsignor Vincent Mackey from Boston, who showed up for almost all the Chiefs' games, home and away. Hank called him "Blackbird," after his priest's black suit. Back in 1969 we beat the Chiefs twice during the season even though the Monsignor was there. But when we played for the AFL championship in Oakland that year, we lost. Virginia and I are Catholics, but she blamed the monsignor.

"What's he doing at football games on Sunday?" she said. "I'm going to write to the Pope about him."

She never did, but Hank had gotten to her. And to me. Hank got to a lot of coaches, but some probably never knew it. Not long ago Hank told me a story about Kansas City's old Municipal Stadium where both benches were on the same side of the field. One of his assistant coach's friends always had a photographer's credentials and a camera. But he never had any film in his camera. He just wanted to watch the game as he walked between the benches. One time he was near the other team's bench when he overheard the coaches talking about throwing a long pass, an "up," to the wide receiver being covered by Jim Marsalis, a Chief cornerback. He hurried over to the Chiefs' bench.

"Watch for the up against Marsalis," he told Hank. "They're gonna throw an up against Marsalis."

Hank and his coaches alerted Marsalis, who knocked down the pass. Whenever he talked about it, Hank would puff with pride at the memory of discovering what the other team was planning. After the Chiefs moved to Arrowhead Stadium, the 1974 Pro Bowl was scheduled there. As the AFC coach that year, I was in a little meeting room going over the game plan with my quarterbacks, Ken Stabler and Bob Griese, when I heard a voice.

"The comeback pass will never work," the voice said.

I realized it was Hank's voice. I don't know where he was, but somehow he could hear me and I could hear him. I talked some more and he kept answering. He obviously had some sort of intercom plugged into that room. He still laughs about that. Hank was always up to something. But that was all right with me. That's the way he was. I could count on Hank being up to something, just like I was every so often. And because Hank was consistent, I enjoyed him just as much as I enjoyed Don Shula for being straightforward.

To me, Don Shula is the best coach of my time. Tom Landry, Chuck Noll, and Bud Grant also have won over a long period—which is the test—but Don has done it with different teams in different cities in different eras.

He won in Baltimore with Johnny Unitas at quarterback, he won there with Earl Morrall at quarterback when Unitas was hurt. He took over a team in Miami that had Larry Csonka and Bob Griese and he won the Super Bowl twice, the first time with a perfect 17–0 season. Then he put together another team that got to Super Bowl XVII with David Woodley at quarterback. Now he's developing Dan Marino at quarterback. He's won with offense, he's won with defense. He's won with Bill Arnsparger as his defensive coordinator, he's won without Arnsparger, who left the Dolphins in 1974 to be the Giants' coach and who left the Dolphins again in 1984 to be the Louisiana State coach.

Against a Shula team, you have to play your best to win. You have to be the better team that day to have a chance.

The most frustrated I ever was as the Raiders' coach was in our 1973 AFC championship game in Miami, a 27–10 loss. The Dolphins would run Larry Csonka inside and we would adjust our defense, but then they would run Mercury Morris outside. Bob Griese even ran a quarterback draw against us. No matter where the Dolphins ran, they never left a Raider unblocked. It seemed like we were never in the right defense. We never got our compass fixed on anything. That game was an example of why Don Shula is such a good game coach, meaning a coach you can seldom get an advantage on. In preparing for some teams you can watch their game films and know that you can do almost anything you want to do almost any time you want to do it. You can keep doing the same thing over and over. But against a team with a good game coach, once you do something, they adjust and you can't do it again. You might find something else that's open but not what was open before.

As good as the Dolphins were in winning their two consecutive Super Bowl rings, I thought my Raiders were just as good. But the Dolphins were better on artificial turf (the Orange Bowl had Poly-Turf then) and we were better on real grass—if only because that's what our home fields were made of.

Early in the 1973 season, remember, we stopped the Dolphins' 18-game winning streak, 12–7, on grass at the University of California's stadium in Berkeley (the A's were using the Oakland Coliseum for baseball at the time). And in the 1974 playoffs, when the Dolphins were hoping to be the first team to win three consecutive Super Bowls, we beat them on grass at the Coliseum, 28–26. They went ahead, 26–21, with only about two minutes left, but then Kenny Stabler put together the best drive I've ever seen. After a kick-off return by Ron Smith put us at our 32, he completed 6 consecutive passes, throwing off-balance to Clarence Davis for 14 yards and the winning touchdown with 26 seconds left.

After a few plays in that drive, I had expected the Dolphins to blitz us, but they didn't. I never asked Don why, but through the years I often phoned him to talk football. He never tried to con me. If he didn't want to tell me something, he always said, "I don't want to tell you." As simple and as straightforward as that. But usually he shared his knowledge. One year at training camp my players were lethargic, so I phoned Don to ask if he had ever had that problem.

"If you want to rest your team," he told me, "you don't have to give 'em time off—just cut down on the physical activity."

I believe Don was the first to use what are known now as walk-throughs, where in practice the players just walk through the plays instead of running hard. But until I talked to him, I knew only one way to coach—go hell-bent. He taught me another way.

In all our years as rivals, I only had one misunderstanding with Don, over a 1969 exhibition game before we really got to know each other. He was still with the Colts and I was a rookie head coach. Before coming to Oakland, the Colts worked out at Cal Poly in San Luis Obispo where one of our part-time coaches, Morrie Schleicher, happened to be attending a teachers' seminar. One day Morrie went over to watch the Colts practice and somebody spotted him. Don phoned me.

"Get your spy out of here," he said.

"Believe me, he's not spying on you," I said. "He's down there as a teacher, he's not there for us."

"He better not be," Don said.

We lost that game, 34–30. Maybe we should have had Morrie spying, but I've always considered spying to be overrated. I never felt anyone spied on my team, and I never spied on anybody else's team. I've heard that spying existed in the AFL's early years. Every time we saw a helicopter near our practice field, we joked that Weeb Ewbank or Sid Gillman had a spy up there, just as Weeb or Sid thought Al Davis had a spy in every helicopter or high-rise building near their practice fields.

But when the film-exchange became dependable, there was no reason for spying. Those game films are all you need—if you get them.

Back in my early years with the Raiders, the AFL didn't enforce the film-exchange rule the way the NFL office does now. My two years as an assistant coach, one of my duties was our film-exchange. When we got our game films on Monday morning, I drove over to the Oakland Airport and air-expressed a copy of the films to our upcoming opponent. I also telexed the receipt number to the opposing team so it would know the films had been sent. Later that day or early the next day I drove back to the airport to pick up our opponent's game-films after they arrived. Nothing annoys a coach more than not receiving an opponent's film on time. I learned that if I wanted to delay a film sent to an Eastern team like the Jets or the Bills, all I had to do was air-express it through Chicago where it always seemed to get lost for a day or two.

"Whatever you do," I always told Eastern teams, "don't send your films to us through Chicago."

Some teams you could depend on. One of the nicest guys I dealt with was Jesse Richardson, the Patriots' defensive line coach who also handled their film-exchange. Back when I was a rookie with the Eagles in 1959, he was a good defensive tackle who played on their NFL championship team the next year. During the 1968 season the Patriots played a game in Denver, then stayed at our training-camp base in Santa Rosa the week before coming down to Oakland to play us. I phoned Jesse to find out when I could expect their Denver film.

"I don't know what to tell you, John," he said. "We only have one film made up."

Most teams had two or three copies made of a game film, but the Patriots were trying to save some money. Jesse checked with Mike Holovak, their coach at the time, and called me back.

"Mike told me to send you our film first," Jesse said. "When you're through with it, send it up to Santa Rosa."

That's cooperation. But with some teams, I learned not to send our film until we got theirs, especially the Chargers. Any film exchange between Oakland and San Diego should be easy. Put the film on one of Pacific Southwest Airlines' non-stop flights between the two California cities and it's there in an hour and a half. But it never quite worked out that way. Sid Gillman didn't trust Al Davis, so Sid wouldn't send the Chargers' films until he got our films. Meanwhile, we weren't about to send our films until we got the Chargers' films. After a day or two, one of us would weaken. But by then the Chargers were blaming Al Davis.

"We know it's not you, John," one of their coaches would say on the phone. "We know Al is trying to screw us."

The funny thing is, Al usually wasn't aware of it. I was the one handling the films.

Then there was the time, my fourth season as head coach, before our first playoff game with the Steelers in 1972, that we never got their films and they never got ours. Both teams just got too stubborn to send them.

Looking back now, maybe that was an omen for one of the roughest rivalries in NFL history.

I like rivalries, the NFL needs more rivalries. I think two weeks in the schedule should be set aside for games featuring rivalries—one week for geographic rivalries (Raiders–Rams, Jets–Giants, Cowboys–Oilers), another week for long-standing or current rivalries outside the usual divisional rivalries. But the best rivalries involve top teams playing for something big, like we were with the Steelers for the 1974, 1975, and 1976 AFC championships. Our rivalry had flared in the 1972 playoffs when the Steelers beat us, 13–7, on Franco Harris's "immaculate reception" for a 60-yard touchdown with 5 seconds left. But as controversial as that play will always be, I think the tone of the rivalry was set the night before. We were staying downtown at the Pittsburgh Hilton. After dinner, I was in the lobby when a screaming, surging crowd of several hundred Steeler fans appeared outside the big glass windows.

"Go upstairs to your rooms," a Pittsburgh policeman

was instructing everybody in the lobby. "If you're stay-ing here, go up to your rooms."

The people outside had attended a downtown rally celebrating the Steelers being in the playoffs for the first time in the forty years of the franchise. Now they had decided to come over to our hotel to hoot us, but the police were guarding the doors to the lobby. I was about to take an elevator up to my room when my tight end, Bob Moore, wobbled into the lobby with blood all over him. He had gone out for a walk and when he tried to return to the hotel, the police had mistaken him for a Steeler fan trying to get into the lobby. Bob had to go to a nearby hospital for stitches in his head. With his bandage, he couldn't put his helmet on the next day. We had lost our tight end, and when we lost the game on that "immaculate reception," a rivalry burst into flame. Several weeks later I had a decision to make. I had been invited to speak at the Dapper Dan dinner in Pittsburgh, and I had accepted.

"But with everything that's happened since then," I said to Virginia one night, "I don't know if I should go."

Mike was sitting with us. Mike was nine then and when I didn't seem to know what to do about the dinner in Pittsburgh, he spoke up.

"You have to go," he said.

"What do you mean I *have* to go," I said. "I don't *have* to go."

"Yes, you do."

"Why?" I said.

"You told the people in Pittsburgh that you were going," he said, "so now you have to go."

"You're right."

From the mouths of babes. If you say you're going

to do something, you do it. You don't back out because you lost a football game on a controversial play, or because your tight end got roughed up. I liked the Steelers, especially Art Rooney, their owner and one of the all-time great guys. He liked me too. Every so often I'd get a letter or a postcard from him. Nothing to do with football, just out of thoughtfulness. If you don't like Art Rooney, you don't like people.

Even so, I wondered what sort of reception I'd get. But everybody in Pittsburgh was nice to me. At the dinner, I was applauded. No boos. When it was my turn to speak, I had some fun with Chuck Noll being honored as Pittsburgh's "man of the year" for getting the Steelers to the AFC championship game.

"God let the Steelers win that game with us," I said, thinking of Franco's touchdown. "The committee wanted to give the award to God but since God couldn't be here, they had to give it to a human being—Chuck."

In later years, our rivalry with the Steelers got so intense, it separated Chuck and me as friends. We say hello now, but that's about it. Back when we were assistant coaches, Chuck with the Colts and me with the Raiders, we arranged our college-scouting trips so that we could drive together. In our early years as head coaches, we remained friends. But when the Raider–Steeler rivalry erupted into George Atkinson suing Chuck for slander for talking about a "criminal element" in the NFL, the competition got the best of our friendship. It's a shame it had to come to that, but in our case it did. I think it's happened with other coaches. Hank Stram and Sid Gillman, to name two. And probably a few others who won't admit it.

That doesn't diminish my admiration for Chuck as a coach. He doesn't get the respect he deserves. When people talk about the best coaches, they mention Shula and Landry and whichever coach has a hot team, but they don't mention Chuck and it seems like they never mentioned Bud Grant of the Vikings.

Bud had different players, different personalities, different styles. But he always adjusted to putting everything together for a winning season. He's the best coach nobody ever talked about. To me, he was up there with Shula, Landry, and Noll. If I were an NFL club owner, I'd like to have any of those four coaches running my team.

I never really got to know Tom Landry until after I stopped coaching. The way the schedule fell, when I was the Raiders' coach, we only played the Cowboys once in the regular season. But in my talks with him for CBS the day before Cowboy games, I've realized that he's truly an amazing man.

Tom is totally different from his image. He's not the robot he appears to be on your TV screen. He's an interesting guy with a great sense of humor. One time the Cowboys were about to play the Eagles after one of the Cowboys' running backs, Ron Springs, had popped off about the Eagles' defense. In one of his meetings, Tom looked over at Tony Dorsett.

"Tony, when you line up for the first play," Tom said, "I want you to point to Ron and tell the Eagles' defense, 'Hey, that's Ron Springs, that's the guy who's been saying all those things about you.'"

Knowing him now, I can understand why, in 1984, Tom was in his twenty-fifth consecutive season as the Cowboys' coach. I thought ten years was long but Tom had been coaching the Cowboys for a *quarter of a century*. The reason is, Tom doesn't worry about things he can't control. Tony Dorsett once had a chest problem. If my best running back had been questionable, I would've been a basket case. But when I asked Tom if Tony would play, he shrugged.

"We'll see how he is in the warmup," he said.

I'm sure Paul Brown was a great coach, but I never knew him back in the 50's when he had those great teams in Cleveland every year. I knew him mostly for putting together the Cincinnati Bengals as an expansion team. In those years with a young team, he did the best job of losing of any coach I've ever seen. He never let the Bengals get blown out, never let them be embarrassed. If you got ahead of the Bengals, he would pull in his horns and play conservatively. He kept the score tight. If the Bengals got a touchdown on a blocked punt or an interception, they suddenly were back in the game. Sometimes they even stole the game. And if the Bengals lost, it seldom was by a big score. He always could tell his players that they weren't there yet, but they were only one touchdown away from the Raiders.

In the seven seasons I coached against Paul Brown, we always had a much better team than the Bengals, but in eight games, they beat us three times. In our five victories, we won once by 20 points, but the other margins were 7, 4, and 3 twice (once in a 1975 playoff, 31–28, his last game as the Bengals' coach).

I've always heard about how intense Paul Brown was, but Don Coryell is the most intense coach I've ever been around. Long before he took over the Chargers, I was his defensive coordinator at San Diego State for three years. His intensity carried over into everything he did. In my years with him, the staff always went out to dinner once a week. But whenever one of us opened the door to get into his little Pinto station wagon, it always stunk.

"Damn it," Don would say, "I forgot to leave the garbage at the corner."

Once or twice we could understand. But this happened almost every week. Don's house was on top of a hill, up from where the garbage truck stopped. On garbage days, he would put the garbage cans in the back of the station wagon to drop off at the corner. But then he would start thinking about football and forget the garbage—until we opened the station wagon that night. Sometimes he even forgot his daughter Mindy was in the car. When she was little, she liked to ride down to the corner at the bottom of the hill, then get out and run back home. But if Don forgot about her being in the back seat, Mindy would never say a word. She loved the ride. Don wouldn't remember he had forgotten to drop her off until he got to the office and noticed her. He'd bring her in and phone his wife.

"I'm sorry, honey," he'd say, "but I forgot Mindy again. Can you please come down and get her?"

One time I was driving Don around California on a recruiting trip. He was dressed up in a tie and jacket, which maybe accounted for the headache he had that morning.

"I'll stop at the drugstore for some aspirin," I said.

"No," he said, "just let me out. I'll run it off."

I drove along slowly while he ran a couple of miles like he had when he was a young boxer. But this time he was running in his good shoes. When he got back in the car, his headache was gone.

On the sidelines, Don glowers in concentration so much, he looks like he's modeling for a headache remedy. But he's not always that intense. One year we were having trouble getting summer jobs for our players in the San Diego area. Suddenly an opening developed at the Pepsi-Cola plant.

"Give that job to Dowhower," he said.

Rod Dowhower had been Don's quarterback at San Diego State, but then he had been cut by the 49ers and now he had returned to San Diego, recently married and without a job.

"He needs that job more than any of our kids," Don said.

Don never forgot his players, even after they couldn't play for him—and that's the test. Don later hired Rod as an assistant coach. From there Rod went to the Bronco and the Cardinal staffs.

My three years at San Diego State, one of our assistant coaches was Joe Gibbs, now the Washington Redskins' coach. My first year there, Joe was a graduate assistant. Don assigned him to defense under me. But when it came time for the Varsity–Alumni game at the end of spring practice, Don put Joe in charge of the alumni team.

"I need your plays, Joe," I said.

"You're not getting our plays."

"You've got to give me your plays," I said. "I've got to draw them up on cards so we can practice against them."

"No," he said.

"Hey, listen, when we play another team, we get their plays off the films. Give me your plays. There's nothing wrong with that."

"No," he said.

"We work together. If you don't give me your plays, you'll never coach another down with me."

"I guess I'll never coach another down," Joe said.

He never gave me the plays, but we remained good friends. We were just two hard-headed guys. As it turned out, he never did coach another down with me. The next season, Don Coryell assigned Joe to offense.

"The only time I ever got fired," Joe says now with a laugh, "John Madden fired me."

Don Coryell went on to coach the Cardinals and the Chargers (where Joe Gibbs was on his staff), so I wound up coaching against the coach who gave me one of my big breaks when he put me on his San Diego State staff. In my ten seasons, I coached against all the best coaches of that era.

One of my biggest disappointments was that I never got to coach against Vince Lombardi. My first year as the Raiders' head coach in 1969 was his first as the Redskins' coach. But before the 1970 season started, Vince Lombardi died of cancer.

My only personal contact with him occurred at the coaches' meeting where we were discussing pass-protection as opposed to holding. Out of respect for the older coaches, I hung back, listening to Weeb Ewbank talk about wanting his fair advantage and then watching the great Lombardi stand up to speak.

"Gentlemen," he began, "I'll tell you what pass-protection is. This is pass-protection. The hands are in here."

He was holding his hands tight against his chest, with both fists clenched, then the textbook way to block for the passer. Holding his hands there, he continued to expound for a few minutes on his theories of pass-blocking, then he sat down. Silence. The other coaches looked around at each other, as if nobody dared to follow him. Except me, who didn't know any better. I had been waiting to talk anyway and now I stood up.

"That may be what pass-protection is to you, Coach Lombardi," I said respectfully, "but that's not what it is to me and that's not what's going on in this game. If you look closely at game-films now, you won't see many pass-blockers doing what you're talking about."

I went on about how an offensive lineman couldn't keep his hands in close to his chest when pass-blocking, that he had to keep his hands out in front of him and use his hands to fight off the pass-rusher. Under the rules then, the pass-blocker couldn't move his hands outside the plane of the pass-rusher, but the pass-blocker had to keep his hands out in front of him if he hoped to be effective, not close to his chest. More and more pass-blockers were using this technique in order to cope with the bigger and quicker pass-rushers. All around me, I could see the other coaches nodding in agreement. When the meeting ended, Vince Lombardi looked over at me.

"John, you're right," he said. "That's what the pass-blockers *are* doing now."

We started to talk football. For the only time in my life as it turned out, I was talking football with Vince Lombardi, just as if I were back in Daly City talking football with John Robinson outside the pool hall. The more we talked, the more I knew I had to ask him a question that had always intrigued me.

"What is there," I said, "that separates a good coach from a bad coach?"

"Knowing what the end result looks like," Vince said. "The best coaches know what the end result looks like, whether it's an offensive play, a defensive coverage, or just some area of the organization. If you don't know what the end result is supposed to look like, you can't get there. All the teams basically do the same things. We all have a draft, we all have a training camp, we all have practices. But the bad coaches don't know what the hell they want. The good coaches do."

After that, whenever I put something new in the Raider playbook, I always tried to picture what the end result should look like. And then I worked to create that end result.

Even though I didn't know Vince Lombardi very well or very long, I treasure my memories of being around him, listening to him. Those older coaches were fun to listen to, even Weeb Ewbank, who was always trying to con everybody. Cherubic little Weeb, you had to trust Weeb—except nobody did. Late in the 1972 season we had already clinched the AFC West when the Jets arrived in Oakland for a Monday night game with a 7–5 record. They had to win to stay in contention for a wild-card playoff berth. Out on the field before the game, Weeb wandered over to talk to me.

"You know, Johnny," he said, "you'd really be better off if we won this game."

I've forgotten Weeb's reasoning, but I remember that we won, 24–16, even though Joe Namath passed for 403 yards. Weeb was always trying to slip something past you. One time before a game at Shea Stadium, where the wind off Flushing Bay would swirl in gusts, we were out warming up when Weeb took me aside.

"Johnny," he said, "I've never told another coach this, but I'm going to tell you because you're my friend."

Weeb pointed to what looked like a long gray rag fluttering from the mezzanine deck behind the goalposts at the closed end where home plate is for baseball.

"The wind is treacherous here," he said, "but the way you tell which way it's blowing is by that gray thing there."

Weeb might as well have bored a hole in my head and put that gray rag in it. I didn't dare tell any of my players, especially my kicker George Blanda, about that gray rag. I didn't want to psyche him the way Weeb had psyched me. But whenever we were moving toward the closed end that day and I started wondering if we might have to settle for a field goal, I thought about that gray rag—but I refused to look at it. For all I knew, Weeb had somebody up there with an electric fan blowing that flag every which way. I just knew that if I looked at it, I'd get taken somehow.

We won that game too, but Weeb had me. And he had what every coach wants—his fair advantage.

14

Differences of Opinion

I SOMETIMES SECOND-GUESS NFL GAME OFFICIALS from the TV booth and I used to yell at them from the sideline when I was coaching. I'm sure some people probably think I don't like officials. But that's not true. Oh, there were a few I didn't like, but I liked almost all of them. I really did. I think they liked me too. We just had an occasional difference of opinion, usually when the Raiders were on the road. That's when I was always on the officials. The home team's crowd was trying to intimidate them, so I tried to balance it.

At a game in Denver once, I really got on Burl Tolar, a head linesman, a good official, and a classy guy. After we won, 27–16, we were in the Denver airport waiting for our chartered jet when I noticed Burl coming along the corridor toward the gate for his flight home. I was about to get on him again until I realized he was looking at me.

"John," he said, smiling, "I just want to say one thing. You're really a beaut."

As he kept on walking toward his gate, I stood there, completely deflated. If he had wanted to argue, I would have argued, but I couldn't argue with that. *You're really a beaut.* That's how the officials were reacting to me my last few seasons as a coach. Humoring me. Almost laughing at me. If one of them was near me after a close call, I would yell at him but he would hardly acknowledge it.

"You're something today," the official might mutter.

They stopped fighting with me, which is the best way to avoid a fight. They had taken me seriously my first few seasons as the Raider coach. But after that, the officials acted like they were just putting up with me, that I was noisy but harmless. In a way they were correct. I lost my temper on the sideline every so often, but I was never out of control. I was just being me. I've always believed that as long as a man is himself and not a phoney, he is never out of control. And when I visited the officials in their dressing room before every game, I was always in control.

"Just a time check," I would say. "I want to make sure my watch has the same time as yours."

I also was in there to make the opposing coach think I was trying to con the officials. Sometimes I was, especially if the other team had been getting away with something that was illegal. Or if that particular crew had made a bad call the last time they had a Raiders game. Just as I was leaving their dressing room, I would remind them about that bad call.

"Remember that interference call in Kansas City six weeks ago?" I might say. "McNally told me you blew that one. Don't let it happen again."

I wanted them to know that I knew that Art McNally, the NFL supervisor of officials, had agreed with me when I had complained to him. I studied the officials. I knew the officials. And sometimes I couldn't help myself from messing with them. Every so often I'd go to their dressing room before they got there and take their sandwiches. One morning at Sunday mass in an Oakland church, four officials were in the pew in front of me. One of them draped his raincoat over the backrest. I couldn't resist the temptation. Not even in church. Just before mass ended, I put the raincoat over my arm as if it were mine, walked back to the vestibule, and tossed it on a chair as I left.

Through the years, the Raiders had so many big games that we usually were assigned the top referees—Tommy Bell, Jim Tunney, Ben Dreith, Pat Haggerty, Norm Schachter.

The worst I ever felt after an incident with an official involved Pat Haggerty, one of the best referees and one of the good guys. We were playing the Bills in a Monday night game in Oakland when Fred Biletnikoff got ejected for fighting. I was really upset. Fred had never had a fight in his life and now he was out of the game. Pat, who was the referee, came over to the sideline to explain to me what had happened. When he walked away, I was so frustrated I reverted to an old streetcorner gesture known as the Italian salute. I didn't mean it for Pat, but on national prime-time TV that's how it looked. The next day I phoned Art McNally.

"When you talk to Pat, please tell him I'm sorry," I said. "I wasn't doing it at him."

Ordinarily, whenever I phoned Art McNally, I was complaining, not apologizing. The only fifteen-yard penalty I ever got as a coach happened in Denver when

I was arguing a fifteen-yard unnecessary-roughness penalty. Jack Tatum had knocked one of the Broncos out of bounds in front of me at midfield. Happened all the time, but Jack Fette, the line judge, dropped his yellow flag. I went crazy. I also went beyond the bounds of propriety. As the ball was being paced off to our 35-yard line, I called Jack a blind bastard. The next thing I knew, he was in front of me again.

"Who," he snapped, "did you call a blind bastard?"

"You, that's who," I roared. "There's only one here and that's you."

Jack threw his flag again. Up in the air this time. It fluttered down in front of me. Unsportsmanlike conduct. Another fifteen yards. Suddenly the Broncos were on our 20 because of the two penalties. I was really wild now, screaming and stomping all over the sideline. It turned out all right. Phil Villapiano intercepted Craig Morton's pass and returned it to midfield, then Kenny Stabler hit Dave Casper for a touchdown in a game we won big, 42–17. But when we were kicking off after that touchdown, referee Norm Schachter was standing near me.

"What was my penalty for?" I yelled.

"Because of what you called Jack," he said. "Not once, but twice."

"The second time, I was just answering his question."

"What do you mean, you were answering his question?"

"He asked me who I had called a blind bastard, and I told him it was him. I was just answering his question. I guess if I'd lied to him, it would've been all right, huh? But he asked me. I told him the truth."

Early the next morning I phoned Art McNally at

the NFL office. I wanted to get him before Jack talked to him.

"Art," I said, "one of the things we have to have in life is honesty. And a man should never be penalized for honesty. But that's what happened to me yesterday. Jack Fette made a bad call: In the heat of battle I told Fette he was a blind bastard, and that was wrong. But after they marched off the fifteen yards for unneces- sary roughness, he came over to me and asked me who I had called a blind bastard. I told him it was him and he hits me with fifteen yards for unsportsmanlike conduct. That's not right, Art. I could have lied and told him I meant somebody else, but I told Jack the truth, I told him it was him I meant. He penalized me for being honest, for telling the truth."

"He shouldn't have penalized you for that," Art told me.

I never heard any more about that call. But there's one call that will always haunt me—the "immaculate reception" by Franco Harris. At Three Rivers Stadium in our 1972 playoff game. We were losing, 6–0, until late in the fourth quarter when Kenny Stabler got away from the Steelers' pass-rush and ran 30 yards for the touchdown that put us ahead, 7–6, with 73 seconds remaining. After we kicked off, Terry Bradshaw com- pleted two passes to the Steelers' 40 but then he mis- fired on his next three passes, all of which Jack Tatum broke up.

Fourth down, 20 seconds left. At the snap, our pass- rush pressured Bradshaw into scrambling, then he threw a pass downfield toward his halfback, Frenchy Fuqua, who went for the ball as Jack Tatum went for him. The ball rebounded off one of them (even after all the films I've seen, I'm still not sure which one).

But I can still see that ball floating back toward Franco, who reached down, caught it at full speed at our 42, and ran untouched into the end zone for a 60-yard touchdown, with 5 seconds showing on the clock. Except that not one of the officials immediately raised his arms to signal a touchdown.

In the confusion, I was shouting at the referee, Fred Swearingen, and so were all my players. So were Chuck Noll and all his players.

Under today's rules, it wouldn't have made any difference which player the ball rebounded off. But at the time, the rules stipulated that if the ball bounced off an offensive player (Fuqua), a teammate was ineligible to catch it; if the ball bounced off a defensive player (Tatum), then Franco was eligible to catch it. Naturally, we were protesting that it had been an illegal touchdown, while the Steelers were yelling that the touchdown should stand.

After the officials huddled in the end zone, Swearingen hurried to the telephone in one of the baseball dugouts.

I learned later that Swearingen talked to Art McNally, who was sitting near a TV monitor in the press box with Jim Kensil, then the NFL's executive director. Because of the TV monitor, Art has been accused of using instant replay to determine whether the ball bounced off Fuqua or Tatum, but Art has always denied that. Art's explanation has always been that, because the play would virtually decide a playoff game, Swearingen wanted to be sure of the rule. Whatever their conversation, after at least thirty seconds, which is a long time when you're waiting for a decision to decide a playoff game, Swearingen popped out of the dugout and raised his arms. Touchdown.

After the kickoff, we had time for one play—a long pass from Stabler to Raymond Chester that the Steelers broke up. We had lost. We were out of the playoffs.

Of all my losing games, this was the most depressing, the most confusing, the most mysterious. If the officials knew it was a touchdown, why didn't they rule it a touchdown immediately? If they didn't know it was a touchdown, how did they discover it was—from instant replay on the TV monitor where Art McNally and Jim Kensil were sitting?

It's still a mystery to me.

Even so, I don't believe the NFL should use instant replay to monitor its officials during a game. No way. Because of the angles involved, the NFL couldn't possibly have enough cameras to be absolutely sure on some calls, especially holding or pass-interference. But for years I've believed that the NFL should amend its rules to protect its quarterbacks more. We need the quarterbacks. There aren't enough to go around.

The so-called quarterback "protection" rules only deal with the passer when he still has the ball. But a quarterback seldom gets hurt when he has the ball. After he has thrown a pass—that's when his ribs are particularly vulnerable.

Defensive players aren't allowed to hit a punter or a place-kicker after he kicks the ball. Defensive players shouldn't be allowed to hit a quarterback after he throws the ball. For years I've suggested that the referee (the guy in the black hat standing behind the quarterback) should have a sound-device similar to a small air-horn. The moment the ball leaves the quarterback's hand, the referee would sound the horn, a signal that the quarterback can't be hit. I'm not talking about a quarterback who runs around. He's fair game. I'm talking about a drop-back quarterback passing out of a pocket. He should have the same protection as a punter or a place-kicker.

I'd also like to see the NFL officials go to a training camp like the teams do. Study the rules, study films. They do that now, on their own and the night before a game with the other officials in their crew, but I think it would be helpful for as many as possible to do it together in a training-camp atmosphere.

I also think the NFL should keep its best officiating crews together through the playoffs and the Super Bowl, not put together special crews of their best referees, umpires, head linesmen, line back judges, and field judges. Mixing officials into new crews can create communication problems. That's what happened in the 1979 AFC championship game at Pittsburgh when wide receiver Mike Renfro of the Oilers caught a pass at the sideline in the end zone that was ruled no touchdown. But for a few moments, there was no call. One official needed help from another official, but he didn't receive any help. After a conference, it was ruled no touchdown. When in doubt, the officials should always confer. If that crew had been together from the start of the season, the officials would have worked together better.

The crew that ruled on the "immaculate reception" at least had a conference. The umpire that day was Pat Harder, a terrific competitor as an official just as I'm told he was a terrific competitor as a fullback and linebacker with the Chicago Cardinals and the Detroit Lions in the years after World War II. As an official, Pat still reacted like a player. I remember seeing him get bowled over accidentally by a tight end. The next time that tight end came near him, Pat elbowed him.

He reacted the same way if anybody yelled at him, so I tried to take another approach.

"I wish all the officials were like you, Pat," I would say. "You understand this game."

One time we were on our way to a 35–13 rout of the Lions, one of Pat's former teams. On a fourth-and-20, they went into punt formation but the fullback took the snap and tried to run for a first down. We stopped him, but Pat dropped his flag. Defensive holding. First down. I was really annoyed, but I knew better than to yell at him. I waited until he was nearby.

"The only reason you called that," I told him quietly, "was that you used to play for the Lions and now they're so bad, you're embarrassed for them and you're trying to help them."

Pat didn't even look at me. But a few plays later, he was near our sideline. He still wouldn't look at me, but he glanced over at Ollie Spencer, our offensive line coach who was standing next to me.

"Hey, Ollie," Pat said, "did you hear what this crazy guy came up with now?"

I liked to talk to the officials, to make sure they were watching the same game I was. Most coaches talk to the officials, especially when the crew comes out on the field before the game. But one time Norm Van Brocklin gave an official the toughest time I've ever seen. We were playing the Atlanta Falcons during the 1974 training-camp strike when almost all our players were rookies. As soon as I saw Dutch on the field during the warmup, he started moaning. He seemed to be taking the strike personally.

"This is awful," he said. "What the hell can you do with just rookies?"

"We're all in the same boat," I said. "The strike will be over pretty soon."

In those years, the officials held the coin-toss half an hour before the game. At the appointed time my captains walked over for the coin-toss. But when none of the Falcon captains were there, one of the officials walked over to where Dutch and I were talking.

"Coach Van Brocklin," he said, "can I have your captains for the coin-toss?"

"You're a rookie official," Dutch yelled. "I don't talk to rookie officials."

"Coach Van Brocklin," the official said, "I just want your captains for the coin-toss."

"I told you I don't talk to rookie officials. Get the hell out of here."

The rookie official didn't know what to do, but he knew he couldn't just stand there listening to Dutch yell at him. By now I had wandered away, but I could hear the rookie official telling the referee what had happened. Soon the referee approached Dutch.

"Just tell him who your captains are?" the referee said.

"I don't have to tell him anything," Dutch said. "I don't talk to rookie officials."

"All right, tell me who your captains are?"

"My captains are on strike," Dutch roared.

The referee didn't know what to do, but I had an idea. "Hey, Dutch," I yelled, "I'll call the coin-toss for you."

"Yeah, you call it," he said.

The referee and I went back to where my Raider captains had been waiting. The referee tossed the coin.

"Heads," I called.

The referee peered down at the coin on the grass. "Heads it is," he said.

"Atlanta will kick off," I said.

Dutch didn't care. At least that day at what was virtually a "rookie" game, he didn't care. But generally speaking, nobody cares about officials' calls more than coaches. Those calls affect which team wins or loses—which means they affect which coaches stay or get fired. Usually an official makes his call and, good or bad, that's it. But once I think I influenced a call. Halfway through the 1970 season we were playing in Kansas City, trailing 17–14 with about a minute left. On third down, quarterback Len Dawson bootlegged to our 29 for an apparent first down, but Ben Davidson wasn't sure if Dawson had been tackled or had fallen.

"If he had fallen," Ben explained later, "he still had to be tackled."

Ben tackled him all right, with a knee as much as anything else. That provoked Otis Taylor of the Chiefs to jump on Ben, which started a melee. When the referee, Bob Finley, got everybody sorted out, he called a fifteen-yard penalty on Ben for unnecessary roughness, which moved the Chiefs to our 14-yard line. He also ejected both Ben and Otis.

"Hey, wait a minute," I yelled, "if you eject Otis, that's an automatic fifteen-yard penalty on him. The two penalties wipe each other out. You have to play the down over again."

None of the officials were listening to me. Or they didn't want to listen. But for once, I knew I was right. I called over Dan Connors, our middle linebacker, who was our defensive captain. I explained my argument to him, then he explained it to Finley and the other officials. To my surprise, Finley looked over at me and nodded.

"Because the play was not yet dead," Finley said later, "the two penalties cancelled each other. The down had to be replayed."

On third down this time, we stopped Ed Podolak short of a first down, then the Chiefs punted into our end zone. Starting from our 20-yard line with 46 seconds left, Daryle Lamonica moved us across midfield. With only three seconds left, George Blanda's field goal salvaged a 17–17 tie. On the other sideline Hank Stram was screaming at the officials. And up in the old stands at Municipal Stadium, the Chiefs' fans were still screaming and booing. Going off the field, I went over to shake hands with Hank.

"Good game, Hank," I said. "Good game."

Hank wouldn't even look at me. He just kept walking off the field. Sometimes it's easy to shake hands, but when the field is filled with spectators, it's almost impossible. At a coaches' meeting later, we decided that if the other coach didn't shake hands or didn't *want* to shake hands, no hard feelings. For a coach, there's nothing so frustrating as a call that takes away a win.

It's especially frustrating when a call is incorrect like the one we had on Rob Lytle's fumble in Denver in the 1977 AFC championship game.

No matter how many times I watch the films of the "immaculate reception" play, I never know for sure what happened. But the play in Denver was different. Films of that play confirmed what I knew had happened—that Rob Lytle of the Broncos had fumbled at our 1-yard line, that Jack Tatum had recovered the fumble, that the Broncos never should have scored a touchdown on the next play for a 14–3 lead midway through the third quarter, and that we never should have lost that game, 20–17.

I knew all that without seeing the films, but the head linesman, Ed Marion, didn't. From where he was, out near the sideline, he didn't see Lytle fumble, he didn't see Tatum recover it for us. Once the Broncos ran their next play, the controversy was over, at least as far as the officials were concerned. On the sideline, I wanted to run out on the field and hold up the game by arguing until the officials realized it was our ball. But what annoyed me is that they never huddled. On the "immaculate reception" play in Pittsburgh, at least the officials had huddled. But in Denver they never did. If they had, I think one of the other officials would have acknowledged that he had seen the fumble. Thousands of people at the game had seen it, millions of people watching TV had seen it. At least one of the six officials had to have seen it.

Even more frustrating, I knew that TV would be showing the replay, I knew the newspapers would have the picture. Which they both did.

I knew everybody would be saying that the Raiders got taken. Which we did. So the Broncos went to Super Bowl XII and we sat home. Maybe the Broncos would have won that AFC championship game anyway. I'll never know. But in 1983, at a CBS seminar for all its producers, directors, and broadcasters at NFL games, Art McNally went over the rules, then he showed film. With each piece of film, he would ask us questions. Is this pass-interference? Is this a legal catch? Is this a fumble? Now he was showing several plays with apparent fumbles, each time asking, "Is this a fumble?" All of a sudden, I heard myself asking a question.

"How about the Rob Lytle play in Denver, the 1977 AFC championship game?" I blurted out. "Was that a fumble?"

I hadn't done it with premeditation, it just popped out. In the darkness of the room, I don't think Art realized John Madden was the one who had asked him the question about the Denver play.

"Yes, the Lytle play," Art said, "that was a fumble."

"Damn it," I said, "where the hell were you when I needed you? That call put the Broncos in the Super Bowl and we went home. That call gave me an ulcer."

By now Art knew it was me. He was laughing along with everybody else in the room.

"I might still be coaching," I said. "I might not even be here at this meeting."

But no, I wouldn't be coaching now, no matter what. I'm not a coach anymore. I'm a TV analyst. I'm a radio commentator. I do Miller Lite commercials. I even did a book.

About the Author

John Madden is a CBS commentator on NFL games. Formerly the head coach of the Oakland Raiders for ten seasons, he lives in Pleasanton, California, with his wife, Virginia. They have two children—Michael and Joseph.

Dave Anderson has been a sports columnist at *The New York Times* since 1971, winning a Pulitzer Prize in 1981 for distinguished commentary. He lives in Tenafly, New Jersey, with his wife, Maureen. They have four children—Stephen, Mark, Mary Jo, and Jean Marie.